Forecasting and Simulating Software Development Projects

Effective Modeling of Kanban & Scrum Projects using Monte-carlo Simulation

Troy Magennis

DEDICATION

To Aiden and Janet – Two reasons my life is wonderful.

CONTENTS

Acknowledgements

Although this book has a single author listed, its preparation was heavily influenced by many people, some of whom I want to call out specifically to acknowledge my gratitude.

Janet Magennis took the major workload of copy-editing my work. I'm prone to long rambling sentences that sometimes never completed; Janet fixed all of these and also my complete lack of consistency in punctuation and style day to day.

Daniel Vacanti is a thought-leader in the Kanban area and it has openly commented on his views about a more mathematical approach to managing software projects and how simulation can achieve the next level of maturity in our industry. He fielded the many a phone call when I wanted to run through some thoughts, and I thank him for his time and passion.

And although it seems cliché, I want to acknowledge you for buying this book. There needs to be more people taking the challenge of improving software project forecasting and management. By buying this book you have shown that you are open to new ideas and ways of working. I hope you send me some feedback and expand on this work by adding and publically discussing your own ideas on how to improve software forecasting.

Troy Magennis,

Seattle. 2011.

Preface

Why This Book Was Written

This book was written because I believe that doubling a software project estimate should not be considered best practice. I've given, and been given estimates on software projects that I knew were wrong and misleading, and participated in doubling what I heard in order to account for "unknowns." I knew there must be a better way and by researching other fields, I found and adapted techniques that make software project forecasting more accurate. These techniques embrace uncertainty and using it as a weapon against poorly considered project timelines and understaffed teams.

The process described in this book explains how to model software development projects, and to use those models to actively manage risk; for example, forecast dates, cost and staff requirements for a proposed project. Modeling and simulating a system provides a level of experimentation that is cost prohibitive to perform in practice. You don't get to play out hundreds of what-if experiments on a real project – you get just one chance to deliver on-time and on-budget. The models we build represent a close facsimile of the real world software development process, the closer facsimile, the more accurate the results and better decisions made on interpreting those results – but as we will see, understanding the impact of each facet of the model helps us put the effort into improving the model (and project) only where that effort will give significant timeline improvement.

This book describes how to model the two most common methods for software development and delivery today, those being iterative based Agile processes based on story-point estimation (think Scrum), and lean processes that are cycle-time estimated (think Kanban). From a modeling and simulation perspective each offers opportunities for answering important questions. It is not the intention of this book to change your development process. Rather, I describe examples from both practices, however, some simulation types lend themselves better to one or the other, and I explain why when that occurs.

Who Should Read This Book

This book is intended for people in the software development industry who are looking for more certainty in the forecasting and staffing of their projects. Because this book also describes the benefit of modeling and what questions can be answered by simulating those models, this book will also be enlightening to executive management for software development organizations.

People with the following responsibilities will find this book of interest –

- *Project Managers*: Understand how to model and forecast projects, and how to simulate those models for answering questions regarding forecasting delivery dates, cost, and staffing needs.

- *Development Managers and Team Leads*: Understand how to reduce the amount of estimation required for delivering forecasts, and how to determine what development events are causing the most impact to delivery.

- *Execute Leadership*: Understand how multiple teams can co-ordinate their forecasts in a methodical way, and provide consistency in how these are generated and reported.

- *Venture Capital Investors*: Understand how to obtain a reliable cost and date forecast for an investment as a primary or secondary opinion.

Chapter Outlines

Chapter 1 outlines the case for modeling and simulating software projects. The reasons why estimates are sought from management and the reasons these questions aren't going away anytime soon.

Chapter 2 is an entertaining look at an example project scenario, demonstrating how modeling and simulation play a key role in from before projects get approved to the ongoing management of those projects. By the end of this chapter you will understand the end-game of simulation and modeling, and have a clearer picture of the answers achievable by using techniques described in this book.

Chapter 3 introduces the basics of statistics and random number theory that will be used throughout this book and your career in modeling and simulating software projects. The mathematics required isn't complex, but the language and style of this book's examples requires an agreed understanding and vocabulary to aid in digestion.

Chapter 4 discusses the estimation techniques required when building models. By utilizing modeling and simulation using the techniques described in this book, the amount of estimation is at its minimum necessary. This chapter describes how to quickly obtain the estimate ranges necessary from experts in systematic fashion to ensure accurate simulation and forecasts.

Chapter 5 introduces the simulation model language, SimML, and shows how to build your first Scrum and Kanban models. By the end of this chapter you will understand the basic structure of a model file, and know how to define the backlog of work and the project structure for Kanban and Scrum project types.

Chapter 6 describes the powerful event definition aspect to SimML models. It is the power of this eventing system that allows accurate simulation of the compounding impact of added scope, defects and blocking events on a forecasted date. Modeling these software project events is what makes building Excel spreadsheets difficult, and the reason SimML is so much more effective at representing real-world probability.

Chapter 7 shows how to simulate the SimML models. This chapter explains how to use the Kanban and Scrum Visualization application to perform visual simulation of a model for initial testing of the model and for showing others static or video demonstrations of the project simulated completion. This chapter also shows how to perform a Monte-carlo simulation of a model and interpret the results.

Chapter 8 is where all of the previous knowledge culminates in performing date and cost forecasts for modeled projects. This chapter explains how to perform forecasts and how to understand the results returned from the simulation engine.

Chapter 9 shows how to analyze the WIP limits and staff of a Kanban model. The staff analysis features of the simulation engine give recommendations of what Kanban column WIP limits to modify in order to reduce the cycle-time or completion time of a modeled system. This chapter gives example of how to find what skills the next hire should have, and how to present those suggestions to management in order to get the right resources on-boarded to complete your projects faster.

Chapter 10 shows how to perform impact analysis on a model. Impact or sensitivity analysis returns a list of what input factors cause the most change in forecast. Managing these most influential factors is the best use of your time, and lead you to make project changes and behavioral changes that most matter.

Chapter 11 looks at how to reverse engineer actual measured data. It shows how to determine if measuring and mining certain data is value for money, and once you determine that a certain measurement is important, how to analyze that data to update the values in your model for more accuracy.

Thank you for being interested in improving the software development process, and I hope you find the journey of modeling and simulating a fulfilling one; one that gets you answers to the questions you have quickly and accurately.

Simulation and Forecasting Software used in this Book

In order to run the examples shown throughout this book you need to download and install the Focused Objective Kanban and Scrum Simulation Visualizer application. As a purchaser of this book you qualify for a free license to experiment and follow along with the examples in this book on your own.

The features of this software are –

- Simulation engine that supports Agile/Scrum projects and Lean/Kanban projects.
- Simulation engine that supports visual (video's), Monte-carlo, forecasting date and cost, and sensitivity analysis commands.
- Model editing application that color codes and groups model code.
- Visual simulation result application window to single-step through a project one day or iteration at a time.
- XML and HTML format reporting for simulation results.
- Summary statistics application that helps reverse engineer existing data for improving model inputs.

Download the Simulation Software and Example Files

The simulation software setup application can be downloaded from –

http://www.focusedobjective.com

The instructions found at this location include system requirements, and how to download and install the application.

Chapter 1
Modeling – Estimation, Forecasting and Risk Management

To set the scene for the rest of the book, this chapter outlines the reasons for and why modeling and simulating software projects is necessary and important. The answers a model can provide go far beyond improved timeline estimates. The ability to quickly test alternative project backlog and staffing structures, and the ability to uncover what factors are most influencing the forecasted results makes modeling critical to success. Modeling is the first step to actively managing all aspects of development process through experimentation via numbers.

What is (numerical) modeling?

Modeling is the art of building an artificial version of an object or process for the purpose of experimentation. Modeling provides a cheaper way to measure the impact of various factors and determine the utility of an object or process without completing that project first. In our case, modeling provides a level of certainty around forecasts of time to complete, the resources required and cost.

A model serves the purpose of understanding the interplay between its various input factors. Determining what factors, and what level of input is required for those factors to cause an artificial failure to occur (an undesirable result, in our case – too long a time or too much cost). Once the model is built, it can be used to predict future outcomes. For example, a *very* simplistic model of a software project is –

```
Work days to complete =
    (Estimated days of work / number of developers) +
    ((Estimated days of work * Defect rate) /
            number of developers)
```

In this example model, the input values of estimated days of work, the number of developers, and a defect rate multiplier (in this model, 0.5 would mean 50% of the work again to account for defects) are combined to forecast the number of workdays. Each input variable has a role to play and impacts the output value. For example, adding developers decreases the result, increasing the defect rate makes the number of days to complete longer. For even this simplest of model, good conversations can be had on the subjects of resourcing and how to decrease defect rates. When this model is expanded to cover more real world occurrences like scope-creep, testing, release management, vacation time, developer skill levels, etc. the model is capable of answering even more complex questions.

Throughout this book, we refer to a model as a tool to allow various analyses to occur on a software development project or portfolio. For the model to work effectively, it needs to be fed enough information to approximate the real world process being mimicked. Many of these input values cannot be fully known in advance, and estimates must be provided; the techniques in this book minimize the need for exact measure by insisting that the likely range (lowest likely, and highest likely) be provided in their place. This allows the model to equate the most likely, with some variation both below and above the most frequent result.

For the moment, think of a model as a mathematical formula. It combines various input values and provides a result. Changing the inputs changes the result. And if one of the inputs isn't known, the formula can be rearranged with a hard-coded result argument in order to solve what that unknown value could be. The ability to continuously perform what-if scenarios in very short time frames is where a model offers a level of understanding of a system far in excess of human intuition (albeit expert opinion) alone.

This book describes how models of software development projects and portfolios can be quickly built and simulated. The results of these simulated "project completions" are assessed in a variety of ways in order to understand and forecast the most likely future outcomes (and some you wish you had never uncovered). It all starts with those important input values which have to be estimated – the single word that strikes fear and loathing into every developer's psyche. Let's cover the broad need for estimation in more detail.

Just Enough Estimation

It is common for estimation to be deemed a waste of time by many participants in the software development process. I have to agree that when playing the role as a developer, I had an adverse opinion as to the need of delaying the start of a project, or stopping the project in order to carry out "another" round of estimation. However, as I made my way into executive management of IT teams and departments, I saw another side to estimates, the one that gets projects approved, and the right number of staff hired. Our aim should always be to do the least amount of estimation possible, and this book describes techniques that get to accurate forecasts with the least amount of estimation distress, arriving at a solution with a desired level of confidence quickly in order for important decisions to occur. I encourage you to keep an open mind on the subject of "estimates are waste" until you see later in this book the types of answers and management techniques possible with just a few estimates.

There are multiple reasons estimation is still important, and this chapter explores the basics of a couple of the major drivers –

1. Choosing the right portfolio of projects, and getting the go-ahead.
2. Planning, hiring and training staff for the future.

Choosing the right portfolio of projects

Most companies don't have a single project idea to build, and even if they do, there is a variety of features and differing opinions as to what features are critical in order to go to market. Choosing which projects get completed and in what order is an important aspect of executive management, but in order to effectively perform this task, these people need some information in which to make decisions.

In larger organizations, the necessity for yearly budgeting is the catalyst for causing all the business stakeholders to present ideas that will allow that company to hit revenue targets in the following year. Sometimes this process is ongoing, with ideas and innovations presented to an "innovation council," at regular times, and those elected on that council to give the nod of approval. All of these approaches for a company managing its new project work require two basic bits of information for each initiative – 1) How much revenue will it make, and 2) How much will it cost. The goal is to understand if the investment being made will reap reward in an acceptable timeframe, often referred to as Return on Investment or ROI. The Return on Investment formula is at its most basic–

```
Return on Investment = Revenue - Cost to develop
```

Revenue (and therefore ROI) is time sensitive, meaning the earlier a feature is in the market earning revenue, the higher the total revenue for the next calendar period. Knowing when a project will be delivered, earning customer revenue is critical to understanding how much cash a given initiative will add to the following years bottom-line. This means that for any considered investment decision, a reliable calendar date estimate of when that feature or innovation will be ready to earn income is necessary, and that is one reason we are constantly asked as developers and program managers to give a delivery date (another being to calculate the cost to develop).

Stepping into your investor shoes for a moment– if you were getting your kitchen remodeled, you would likely want an up-front estimate (and certainly from more than one) vendor in order to make a buy decision. Very few major investments in life occur with the buyer not getting a cost estimate. And software development should be added to that list. I fully understand the concept of Agile getting features to market incrementally, bringing the return on investment earlier, but when needing to make a go/no-go decision and to choose between multiple options- an estimate of the costs involved is necessary before work starts. The return on investment is going to be necessary to ensure that the right projects get started – the projects that improve the bottom line the most.

If the development team isn't given the task to estimate an idea, or are unwilling to do so, SOMEONE ELSE will do it for them. I can't stress this point enough, being proactive in getting the business estimates is key to NOT having someone else form an opinion of how long you will take to do your work. Nobody wants that to occur, but if you had to choose from a portfolio of fifty ideas, and cull them down to ten that will get the go-ahead for the next year (and form the basis of staffing and budget allocation), you would need to know the cost side of the equation.

Another disturbing trend that can cause the wrong projects to progress through the investment phase is the continual doubling of estimates. After being asked for an estimate, it's not uncommon for the person presenting those estimates to add a buffer, a clumsy and often random approach to managing risk. This means that in some cases, the cost of a very minor change, balloons into a major project; or a well estimated initiative gets shelved due to the perceived excessive cost. Doubling the value given is a common approach, and whilst this might bring poorly estimated projects into a more real-world estimate, I'd prefer to improve the estimation process, rather than just accept it as flawed and make an in-accurate estimate more in-accurate. I've seen the doubling approach cause major loss of trust between the business folks and the IT department through ludicrous doubling on doubling of numbers making a minor change a three-month project (the project manager doubled the developer estimate, and the business owner doubled all estimates again when they rolled up all projects – nothing gets approved).

The real goal of estimation is to arrive at an estimate, within an agreed accuracy, in as short a time and minimal staff disruption as possible. This is where modeling and simulating a project is key, and the purpose of the remainder of this book.

Planning, hiring and training staff for the future

Another area where estimation occurs is planning staffing levels for the future. There are always exceptions, but most companies need to match the size of their teams to the amount of work forecast for the future period. Some of this team is required to maintain business as usual, and some of the team is for new features and products, and some of this team is overhead – people required for the organization to continue operation.

The number of staff maintaining business as usual might be thought of as static; but even existing products go through phases of updates, or are impacted by traffic growth that might require remediation work. Somebody has to match supply and demand of these resources, and ensure that the right capacity is available for both the current and future plans. Sometimes future product plans require new skills to be introduced, and making sure the current staff up-skill ready to meet those demands is an important part of being an effective manager. To manage this process, an understanding of the throughput capacity of the team, and the impact of the upcoming tasks on that team needs to be continuously estimated and managed.

Having a model of the team and its throughput is the first step in understanding the hiring needs when demand exceeds supply. Quickly being positioned to know how many and what skills are needed to hire is one of the key management skills required to be effective long-term in the software industry.

When evaluating new projects, the ability to model and provide a resourcing plan is the key element in providing a cost budget. Salary or external contracting costs traditionally are the biggest cost in a software development project. Turning developer estimates into a resource plan that achieves a desired delivery date is the essential element for the cost side of the return on investment equation (as mentioned in the choosing the right portfolio of projects section previously).

Building a resource plan isn't just the number of developers. Designers, testers, operations and release staff are only a few of the other team members required to deliver any software. The resource plan has to match the supply for each area of expertise with the demand for the project, and scale the team in order to bring delivery into a desired date range. For example, a project might define three feature teams (three parallel teams to do work); on each feature team there would be a designer, three developers and a tester. To release the product earlier, a decision might be to add an additional feature team – five people. Finding the right balance will be very project and team member experience dependent. Modeling that team and using simulation to determine the correct balance and impact of adding more staff is a key technique explained now and expanded on later in this book (see Chapter 9).

Forecasting – Staff, dates, revenue and costs

Forecasting is calculating in advance the condition or occurrence of some aspect – in the case of software development, most commonly staff, delivery date, cost and revenue. Estimation plays a role in understanding magnitude of each element, but forecasting combines these many elements into a single unit of measure; either time, or money (or both). Reliable forecasting requires understanding the factors influencing a final result, and accounting for each of them with educated estimates. The more factors you miss, the less accurate (or uncertain) the forecast. When as many as practical factors are combined using estimates for a software project and modeled, the simulation output can be relied upon to give accurate forecasts.

Turning a software feature estimate (or set of estimates) into a delivery date is one forecasting example. Knowing the starting date, the teams size and structure, and the number of days to design, build, test and release a feature allows us to calculate a delivery "live" date. However, more factors are at play, for example, accounting for public holidays, fixed release date windows, a third party delivering a new logo-design, are just some additional factors that might impact the forecast date. *In the end, for managing the ROI calculation, nobody cares deeply about the estimate – it's the forecast that really matters* (but to get to the forecast we need the estimate), and the forecast combines all factors rolling up the results to a final cost or date.

Calculating the move from estimates to a forecast quickly gets complex, and beyond the human scope to solve intuitively (although we try). The interplay between factors, and the flow-on impact of small events early in a project cause major shifts in release date and costs. This gives the illusion that it's a problem too hard to reliably solve, but the process is more understood than first thought. Tools and techniques are available that solve similarly hard problems in other domains, and this book describes an approach using custom tools built for the purpose of forecasting software development projects.

Accurate forecasting is possible and necessary. This book describes the techniques for achieving accurate forecast of software deliver and cost, and how to use those forecasts in decision making.

Risk Management - Forecasting and avoiding disaster(s)

Forecasting has a level of uncertainty. Any forecast does, just ask any meteorologist you might know and sympathize with them; they must get cornered at every party gathering and hounded by those assembled as to why they get the forecast wrong so often. Weather forecasting tries to model mother-nature, and apply current observations with historical trends to predict the future state of environmental climate. Software doesn't get impacted by natural events (mostly – baring the occasional natural disaster like earthquake or flooding of the server room), although some events that occur seem wildly random. For the most part, there are a finite number of events and those events have a range of possible values with fairly narrow upper and lower bounds. In essence, forecasting software delivery is much easier than weather, and we should continue to get better at both. Just like weather forecasting, the closer to the date being forecast, the more likely an accurate result. Both types of forecasting incur greater uncertainty as the time horizon is extended due to the ripple and knock-on effect of early variations in inputs. To reliably model software development (and weather), the model must embrace and simulate how early events combine and influence the longer term results.

Risk management can be broadly defined as the identification, assessment, and prioritization of risks followed up by managing and monitoring those risks in a project (Wikipedia). I also like the definition given in the ISO 31000 standard as "the effect of uncertainty on objectives, whether positive or negative". For our purposes, managing the estimate and forecast risk so that better decisions are made on project we are involved is another plausible definition. It is our job to include risks in our modeling of software projects and to always clearly state the uncertainty of our forecasts so that other people can manage and monitor their risks, and make more informed decisions.

The uncertainty of a model is the range of outputs for a forecast when the input estimates are at their combined worst or combined best. Different levels of uncertainty are appropriate at different times – in portfolio planning, an estimate plus or minus one month might be okay when comparing a few options. However, this range of uncertainty is a deal-breaker to the plan if the cost of failure (not meeting a date for instance that causes missing a legal requirement and incurring fines) is excessive. Risk has a common index equation that helps assess and prioritize the most impactful, most probably risk events first –

```
Composite Risk Index = Impact of event x Probability of Occurrence
```

This formula works simply by getting participants to identify potential risk events, and then allocate a 1 to 5 point value to both the impact (1 = low impact, 5 = major impact) and occurrence probability (1 = very unlikely, 5 = almost certain). These values are multiplied together and the results sorted highest to lowest, assisting in prioritizing the most likely and the most impactful risks to those first managed. I believe this method whilst better than none at all is a far cry from what is possible and necessary, and I'm not alone. Douglas Hubbard in his un-diplomatic book, The Failure of Risk Management: Why It's Broken and How to Fix It (Hubbard, 2009), presents a passionate argument that most methods for managing risk are less than useless and actually cause harm, likening them to "no better than Astrology." He goes onto describe scientific, quantative methods to manage risk, such as Monte-carlo simulation that this book and the tools it describes are based. I obviously agree with his findings, and whilst not wanting to go to the extreme to recommend disbanding any current risk management program relating to software development (or other endeavor), I do recommend understanding and applying the risk management methods describe throughout this book – primarily, modeling and simulating a system.

Modeling and simulating a system doesn't directly estimate a risk index. Once a model is produced, it is possible to directly simulate the impact of one risk occurrence versus another and compare that to all other risks. For example, it may not be clear upfront what the impact is of losing a certain number of staff members, or what the impact is of outsourcing one particular skillset. With a model of the software development process, it is possible to simulate both occurrences and compare that to a baseline simulation forecast on cost and deliver date. The results of this experiment will yield more powerful information in which to make a decision as to how much effort to invest in avoiding (or embracing) those events or strategies. Traditional risk management might highlight an event, whereas modeling and simulation highlight and give magnitude and levity to an event.

Later in this book we carefully look at how to find what factors most influence a forecast, a process called sensitivity analysis. Putting you in the position to constantly know and manage the most impactful elements in a system (in this case a software product or portfolio) is a key goal and purpose of this book and the techniques and tools it describes. I know it sounds like nirvana and a pipe dream at the moment, but the techniques are proven and frequently used in other adventurous fields (finance and mineral exploration for example).

Managing Development Teams and Projects

Good managers set clear goals for their teams. Clear goals are shared ambitions that a manager puts in place by describing the need, the solution and a way to know if progress towards hitting that target solution is being made. A shared vision is a starting point, and too often, team members don't have access to, or don't get visibility into the underlying reasons for a certain goal.

Modeling a system allows impact to be demonstrated, proven and therefore communicated earnestly to staff. Factors impacting the forecast can be identified and managed early if the actual occurrence rates or size are in excess of that initially modeled. Reality will diverge from the model from time-to-time, and in these cases, the model is the starting point to a necessary conversation. In some cases, the model needs changing, but this is a fact to be celebrated! If the change has significant impact on one of the promised forecasts, action can be taken earlier. This divergence also makes the next model more accurate, and these lessons foster an environment of true understand of the entire software development system as a whole – meaning fewer surprises occur in future projects.

The ability to demonstrate that one aspect of the model is having a greater impact than another helps change team behavior. For example, when seeing that a certain type of production defect (say, development environment URL's being promoted to production) is the highest hitter on a sensitivity analysis (a simulation that ranks what inputs have the most influence on a forecast), the team can quickly grasp that it isn't just management inventing problems to solve, the simulated model based on real-world occurrence rates is demonstrating a clear massive impact on a final delivery date. It is often abstract for all team members to be on the same page with respect to how such little problems cascade and grow into weeks or months of delay, but with a model, it can be shown to them. Once understood by the team, setting a target of halving the occurrence rate by the next iteration is a much easier sell.

When using the techniques described in this book, I've found managing my team-leads more effective. Our one on ones are often looking at the model, comparing actual data (occurrence rates and estimates of blocking issues and defects), and discussing any departure. Once we identify a significant departure of model from reality, we agree on whether the model needs to be changed, or the departure managed by the team to bring it back into the model's range. These meetings are some of the most productive meetings I have had (and I hate meetings), Often I walked away learning more about my teams and the factors faced by my development organization than days of retrospectives.

Modeling and simulation offer an opportunity to connect and influence your teams in ways that are non-confrontational and productive. This book describes the techniques to model a system development process and then by comparing actual measured data, identify problems, find solutions and then set targets to make hitting forecasts the most likely outcome.

Summary

This chapter outlined the reasons for modeling and what the benefit is for all team and management members. The answers a model provides go far beyond improved timeline estimates. A model helps all stakeholders understand the impact of their field of expertise and influence on others. Uncovering what factors are most influencing cost, revenue recognition, staffing size and delays, is the first step to actively managing those aspects to hit a goal.

Chapter 2
Example Modeling and Forecasting Scenario

This scenario is for a hypothetical project that aims to re-launch a website. It demonstrates the thinking process and practical implementation of using modeling to quickly forecast staffing levels, go-live dates, and how to interact with senior management to get good decisions made. At the moment, you may not understand all of the terminology and the software used to generate the reports; we cover this material later in the book. This scenario is one of any number of ways of estimating, modeling and forecasting a software project. It's meant to spark your creativity.

The Cast

You – You have the job of managing a team to produce and re-launch the next generation website that will save "The Company."

Charlie – Your CTO. He holds the keys to the budget for staffing requests.

Boris – Your business owner. He has the grand vision and the ear of the CEO.

Your Team – A group of Graphic designers, web developers, server-side developers and testers. At the moment, the exact number of resources you need isn't clear. You have a core group already consisting of -

> 1 – Graphic Designer
> 2 – Web Developers
> 3 – Java Developers
> 1 - QA Engineer

Forecasting Staff and Dates – Getting the Go-Ahead

Your project is one of three options for next year's budget the CEO is considering. He likes all of them and has asked for a better view on the cost of development and the delivery forecasts. The CEO wants a new website to go live before the end of the calendar year. Rumors are your major competitor has a new site to launch end of Q1 next year, and the CEO wants to beat them to it. He also wants to limit investment to $250K in labor costs.

You need to get a cost and delivery date forecast quickly to answer these questions. The first step is to gather the information needed without disrupting the development teams current project. You need to quickly generate the following numbers –

1. Staffing estimate in order to hit at least a partial deliverable by end of calendar year
2. Cost estimate to deliver (forecast)
3. Probability of hitting certain dates (forecast)

   Note:

   Appendix A is listing of the full SimML model file.

Act 1 – Backlog segmentation and Kanban Board Design

To begin, you need a backlog of work to model and estimate. Reviewing the initial backlog of 31 stories you have been given, and roughly modeling defects and blocking events using occurrence data from prior projects, you run a quick forecast date simulation with a very basic Kanban board definition and cycle-time estimates (as shown in Figure 2-1). You want to see how close to January 1st the most basic of simulation model gets you.

Figure 2-1
Basic starting point for Kanban board and estimation.

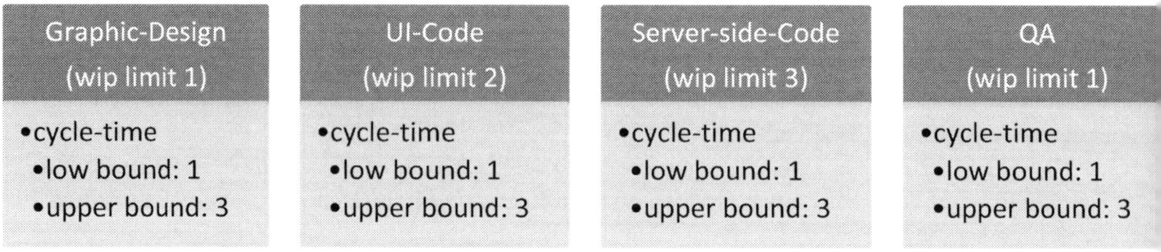

You execute a forecast date simulation run for 31 backlog stories. Listing 2-1 shows the SimML code that performs a Monte-carlo simulation and extrapolates the completion date, and likelihood percentage of hitting that date, and a simple cost estimate (simple estimate ($100K / 52 / 5) x number of staff, now 7). The results of this simulation are shown in Output 2-1.

Listing 2-1

SimML command to run a forecast date simulation.

```
<execute  deliverables="Must-Haves"  dateFormat="ddMMMyyyy">
   <forecastDate  startDate="01Oct2011" intervalsToOneDay="1"
     workDays="monday,tuesday,wednesday,thursday,friday"
     costPerDay="2700" />
</execute>
```

Output 2-1 clearly shows you have your work cut-out for you to deliver by the beginning of the year, and the cost is high, your target is around $250K. At the moment, you only feel confident in saying March 1st, which is approximately your 95th percentile result.

Output 2-1

Most basic simulation of 31 stories using default column cycle-time.

```
<forecastDate startDate="01Oct2011" intervalsToOneDay="1"
      workdays="monday,tuesday,wednesday,thursday,friday"
      costPerDay="2700"  >
  <dates>
    <date intervals="96" date="13Feb2012"
          likelihood="1.60 %" cost="$259,200.00" />
    ...... removed from brevity ......
    <date intervals="108" date="29Feb2012"
          likelihood="92.00 %" cost="$291,600.00" />
    <date intervals="109" date="01Mar2012"
          likelihood="94.80 %" cost="$294,300.00" />
    <date intervals="110" date="02Mar2012"
          likelihood="98.40 %" cost="$297,000.00" />
    <date intervals="111" date="05Mar2012"
          likelihood="99.20 %" cost="$299,700.00" />
    <date intervals="112" date="06Mar2012"
          likelihood="99.60 %" cost="$302,400.00" />
    <date intervals="113" date="07Mar2012"
          likelihood="100.00 %" cost="$305,100.00" />
  </dates>
</forecastDate>
```

You work with Boris, and segment the backlog into two deliverables: Must-Haves, and Everything-Remaining. You then work with your developers and partition each group further. You make a fast pass through the stories and put them into one of four categories-

1. *Small*: Those stories that are possibly under a days work, but certainly less than 2 days work in each column.

2. *Medium*: Those stories that are more than 2 days work but less than 3 days.

3. *UI-Intensive*: Those stories where lots of graphics design and UI coding is necessary.

4. *Server-Side-Intensive*: Those stories where lots of Java service (or .NET, we are all friends here) code is required.

Table 2-1

Estimates grouped by deliverable and then by size and skill specialty.

Delivery Group		
Must-haves	**Developer Estimate Group**	**Number of Stories**
	Small	6
	Medium	4
	UI-Intensive	5
	Server-side Intensive	6

Everything-remaining	Developer Estimate Group	Number of Stories
	Small	2
	Medium	3
	UI-Intensive	2
	Server-side Intensive	3

Act 2 – Cycle-time estimates

For each of the story categories you ask the development team to come up with 90th percentile ranges for cycle time, meaning the cycle-time they feel the actual cycle-time is between the range they give (5% below, 5% above). The final model for Kanban columns and the cycle-times is shown in Figure 2-2.

Figure 2-2
Final Kanban columns, Wip limits and cycle-time estimates for the backlog groups

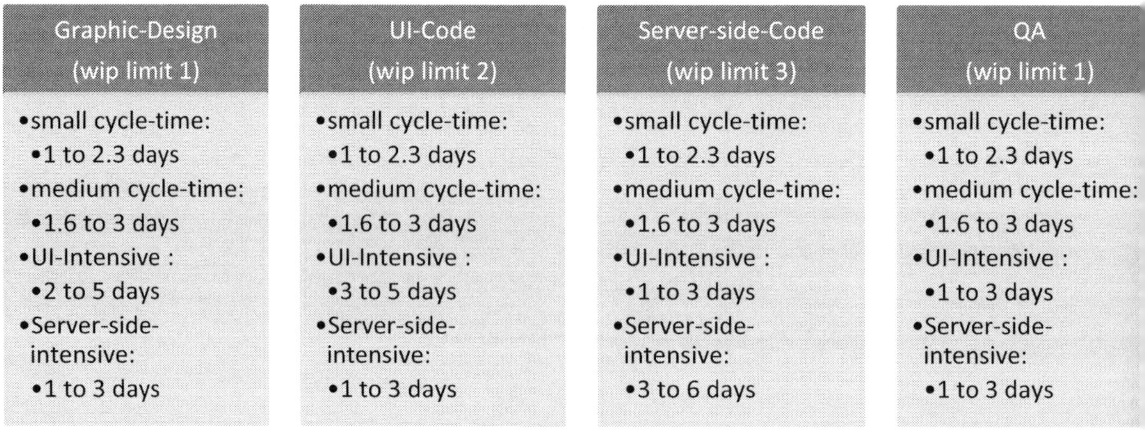

Graphic-Design (wip limit 1)	UI-Code (wip limit 2)	Server-side-Code (wip limit 3)	QA (wip limit 1)
•small cycle-time: •1 to 2.3 days •medium cycle-time: •1.6 to 3 days •UI-Intensive : •2 to 5 days •Server-side-intensive: •1 to 3 days	•small cycle-time: •1 to 2.3 days •medium cycle-time: •1.6 to 3 days •UI-Intensive : •3 to 5 days •Server-side-intensive: •1 to 3 days	•small cycle-time: •1 to 2.3 days •medium cycle-time: •1.6 to 3 days •UI-Intensive : •1 to 3 days •Server-side-intensive: •3 to 6 days	•small cycle-time: •1 to 2.3 days •medium cycle-time: •1.6 to 3 days •UI-Intensive : •1 to 3 days •Server-side-intensive: •1 to 3 days

With this story partitioning, and estimated cycle-times for each category of story in each Kanban column, you look at the forecast for just the "Must-Have" group.

```
<date  intervals="83"  date="25Jan2012"
       likelihood="94.80 %" cost="$224,100.00" />
<date  intervals="84"  date="26Jan2012"
       likelihood="96.80 %" cost="$226,800.00" />
```

Act 3 – Staff tuning to bring in the date

You are still beyond the target date needed to get a go-ahead. You must find what extra staff will bring that date into range. You perform a staff sensitivity simulation on the model (called the `addStaff` command in SimML) and find what it recommends. Listing 2-2 shows the SimML command to determine what the best three column WIP limit changes have the most impact.

Listing 2-2

SimML command to find what staff additions make the most impact to delivery time. In this case, 3 staff recommendations will be made, and every Kanban column can be changed.

```
<addStaff count="3" cycles="250" />
```

The `addStaff` simulation makes three recommendations, add a Graphics Designer, a QA engineer and then a UI Coder in that order. The recommendations are cumulative, and you notice that there is only a marginal benefit in adding the UI coder which is an expensive resource, so you decide not to add that resource. This simulation expected a 34% improvement (reduction) in intervals (days for this simulation).

Output 2-2

Results table for staff simulation. Improvements are cumulative, and improvement is over the original baseline.

WIP Suggestion	Graphics-Design by 1	the QA by 1	then UI-Code by 1
Original WIP	1	1	2
New WIP	2	2	3
Intervals to completion (original 78 intervals)	72	51	47
Cumulative Interval Improvement	7.3%	34.95%	40.68%

Figure 2-3

Simulation chart for recommendations of adding 3 people. Days to completion drop from 78, to 72, to 51, to 47.

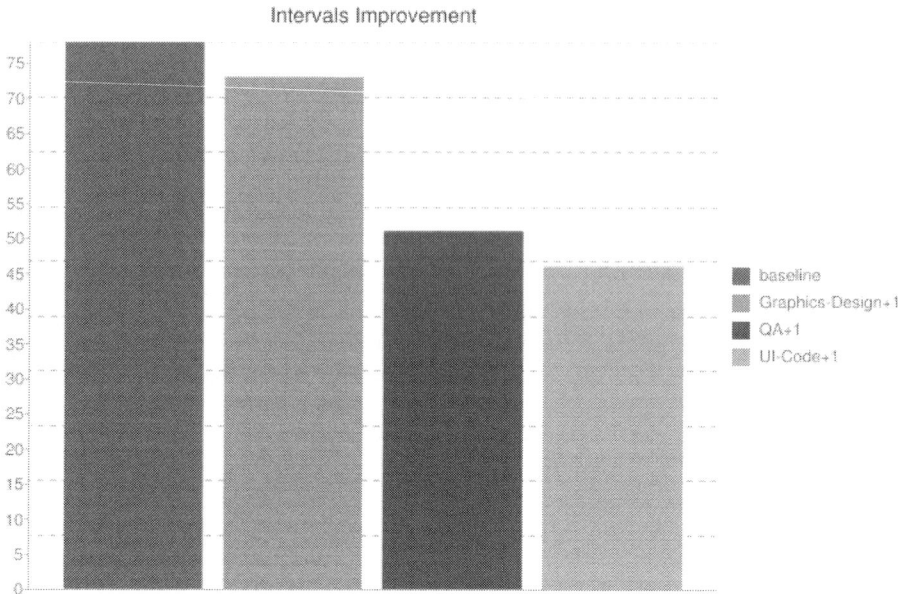

Act 4 – Success; Getting to go-ahead

With the results from Output 2-2 and Figure 2-3 you re-run the forecast date simulation with increased column WIP's for Graphics Design and QA. In order to forecast the extra cost, you must increase the per day cost burn rate by 2 staff as well (using the same formula as before (\$100K / 52 / 5) x number of staff, now 9). You present your findings to Charlie (the CTO) and get the approval to borrow a designer and add a QA engineer if your project gets the go-ahead.

Listing 2-3

SimML command for forecasting completion date with extra resources, and an increase in per-day cost to account for funding those resources.

```
<forecastDate cycles="250" startDate="01Oct2011"
    intervalsToOneDay="1"
    workDays="monday,tuesday,wednesday,thursday,friday"
    costPerDay="3461" />
```

By simulating the SimML command as shown in Listing 2-3, it is now possible to hit the end-of-year target with just the Must-Haves (a scenario Boris supports) with a very high degree of certainty as shown in Output 2-3.

Output 2-3

Forecast date estimate with the extra staff accounted for. This is for the Must-Haves ONLY. You can deliver before end-of year.

```
<date  intervals="54"  date="15Dec2011"
       likelihood="94.00 %" cost="$186,894.00" />
<date  intervals="55"  date="16Dec2011"
       likelihood="95.60 %" cost="$190,355.00" />
<date  intervals="56"  date="19Dec2011"
       likelihood="98.40 %" cost="$193,816.00" />
<date  intervals="57"  date="20Dec2011"
       likelihood="100.00 %" cost="$197,277.00" />
```

To deliver the entire project, you also feel confident in delivering by mid-January, and the total cost of very close to the $250K investment target as shown in Output 2-4.

Output 2-4

Forecast date estimate with the extra staff accounted for. This is for the entire project. Cost is now in-line with expectations.

```
<date  intervals="72"  date="10Jan2012"
       likelihood="94.00 %" cost="$249,192.00" />
<date  intervals="73"  date="11Jan2012"
       likelihood="97.20 %" cost="$252,653.00" />
<date  intervals="74"  date="12Jan2012"
       likelihood="98.80 %" cost="$256,114.00" />
<date  intervals="75"  date="13Jan2012"
       likelihood="100.00 %" cost="$259,575.00" />
```

Boris and Charlie present the business case to the CEO. The CEO is pleasantly surprised that not only did you hit the targets he asked for; he can see that there was method to the calculations and trusts that you can manage to those numbers. Your project gets the go ahead.

From the developers' perspective, they gave a total of 4 estimates of cycle-time, and a single pass through the backlog categorizing the work. They thank you for not having to estimate all 31 stories, and then re-estimate them again when the target wasn't achieved.

Hitting a Date Promised

The project has now been underway, and ten stories have been completed. It's time to make sure that your project is tracking to the model by comparing actual data versus the model's estimates.

Act 5 – Comparing Actual versus modeled

After the first month and a half, actual data can and should be used to refine the cycle-time estimates. The original estimates were very wide in order to capture the group's consensus quickly on what the 90th percentile range would be. Now with a number of stories completed, with a variety of things that went well, and things that went wrong, a narrower range is likely to emerge.

The first step of analyzing actual data is to confirm that the actuals fell within the ranges estimated for cycle-time. Table 2-1 lists the cycle times estimated by the developers, and as you can see in Table 2-2 there were three actuals that fell outside of that range. A 5% variance above or below the range expected for 40 samples would be 2 stories above and 2 stories below; the actuals are showing 2 cards above, which is on the line, but within the bounds, and 1 card below, which is also below the 5% limit. It is too early to be making changes, but keeping an eye on the Medium category cycle-time is in order, another cycle-time above the limit would mean you should increase the cycle-times for simulation.

Table 2-2

Actual column cycle-times for the project after the first 10 stories. 3 cells fell outside of the range estimated.

Story	Delivery Group	Dev. Estimate Group	Cycle-Time Actuals			
			Graphics Design	UI Code	Server Side Code	QA
Story 1	Must-Haves	Small	2.21	0.97	1.22	2.13
Story 2	Must-Haves	UI-Intensive	4.28	4.11	1.23	1.31
Story 3	Must-Haves	Medium	2.26	**0.89**	**1.39**	1.73
Story 4	Must-Haves	UI-Intensive	2.47	3.77	1.22	1.38
Story 5	Must-Haves	Server-Side-Intensive	1.84	1.99	5.30	1.93
Story 6	Must-Haves	Small	1.34	1.24	1.34	1.44
Story 7	Must-Haves	Server-Side-Intensive	1.99	1.85	5.08	2.36
Story 8	Must-Haves	Small	1.78	**3.08**	1.77	1.63
Story 9	Must-Haves	UI-Intensive	3.91	3.24	1.63	1.50
Story 10	Must-Haves	Medium	2.37	1.66	1.83	1.71

Defect rates and blocking event rates do not look as promising. The original estimates in the model compared to actual are shown in Table 2-3. UI Defects are occurring every story. This is twice the rate expected, and is impacting the delivery date.

Table 2-3

Defect and blocking event estimate versus actual occurrence rates after 10 stories.

	Occurrence Estimate	Occurrence Actual
UI Defect	1 in 2 to 3 stories	**1 in 1 (10 so far out of 10 stories)**
Server-side Defect	1 in 3 to 6 stories	1 in 5 (2 so far out of 10 stories)
Block Spec Question	1 in 5 to 10 stories	1 in 3 (3 so far out of 10 stories)
Block Testing Environment	1 in 4 to 8 stories	1 in 5 (2 so far out of 10 stories)

Act 6 – Rallying the Team to Reduce Defect Rates

When you initially modeled your project, you took the defect rates and the blocking event rates from a previous project. You have identified by comparing actual data on this project that one of your defect types, specifically UI related defects is occurring more often than you modeled.

Listing 2-4

SimML model for the UI Defect definition where actual occurrence is once in every story.

```
<!-- Originally modeled UI defects, found in QA, fixed in UI Dev-->
<defect columnId="4" startsInColumnId="2"
        occurrenceLowBound="2" occurrenceHighBound="3">UI Defect
</defect>
<!-- New model based on actual occurrence rates -->
<defect columnId="4" startsInColumnId="2"
        occurrenceLowBound="1" occurrenceHighBound="1">UI Defect
</defect>
```

You update your model definition for this defect from once in every 2 to 3 stories to once every 1 story, matching the actual measured occurrence rate you are seeing from the project. Running a date forecast simulation using this new definition for the Must Haves delivery group shows you will miss the end of year target as shown in Output 2-5.

Output 2-5

New date forecast showing the impact of the UI Defects.

```
<date intervals="66" date="02Jan2012"
      likelihood="93.20 %" cost="$228,426.00" />
<date intervals="67" date="03Jan2012"
      likelihood="97.60 %" cost="$231,887.00" />
<date intervals="68" date="04Jan2012"
      likelihood="98.40 %" cost="$235,348.00" />
<date intervals="69" date="05Jan2012"
      likelihood="99.60 %" cost="$238,809.00" />
<date intervals="71" date="09Jan2012"
      likelihood="100.00 %" cost="$245,731.00" />
```

You pull your team together and explain the observation of UI defects. You share the new date forecast and show them the visual video simulation of the Kanban flow as seen in Figure 2-4.

Figure 2-4
Video screenshot of simulation showing the team the impact of the defects on throughput.

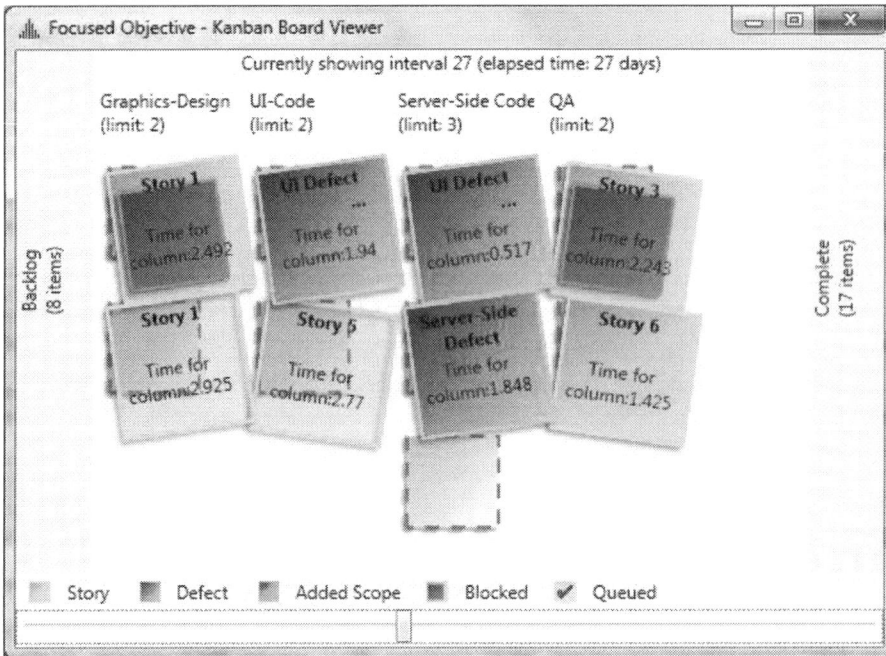

You then demonstrate that adding a **full day to the cycle-time of every story in the UI-Code** column has less impact than the UI Defects currently are causing (as shown in Output 2-6).

Output 2-6

Impacts of increasing the cycle-time for UI-Dev by 1 day (lower and upper bounds). Less than the impact of UI Defects alone!

```
<date intervals="62" date="27Dec2011"
     likelihood="94.40 %" cost="$214,582.00" />
<date intervals="63" date="28Dec2011"
     likelihood="96.80 %" cost="$218,043.00" />
<date intervals="64" date="29Dec2011"
     likelihood="99.60 %" cost="$221,504.00" />
<date intervals="66" date="02Jan2012"
     likelihood="100.00 %" cost="$228,426.00" />
```

On seeing and understanding the impact of these defects, the team brainstorms ideas on how to bring the occurrence rate back into the once every 2 to 3 stories. Their ideas of giving the business owner (Boris) a demonstration and feedback before checking in, getting a peer-review, and spending an extra half-day testing the stories themselves are effective and occurrence rates return to those expected over the next few stories.

> **Note**
> Being able to show that working slower and more carefully (by not
> allowing defects to be raised in later columns) WILL reduce the

overall project time is a key lesson. Although most of this scenario is contrived, this lesson isn't – spend an extra half a day testing during development, as this case shows, even if you spent a day testing you would still be better off than allowing the UI defect rate be high.

Act 7 - What if we added staff now?

Charlie the CTO in your weekly meeting asks you if you want more staff to make sure you reach the promised delivery date. He offers as many developers as you need. You perform an add staff simulation (results shown in Output 2-7), and demonstrate that whilst adding one UI Developer would be the most benefit right now, an additional Graphics Designer and QA Engineer are then next in line most beneficial to throughput.

Output 2-7

The results of an addStaff SimML command showing the next three staff additions that have most impact on reducing days of work.

```
<wipSuggestion  column="UI-Code" originalWip="2" newWip="3"
                intervalImprovement="9.45" >
<wipSuggestion  column="Graphics-Design" originalWip="2" newWip="3"
                intervalImprovement="14.78">
<wipSuggestion  column="QA" originalWip="2" newWip="3"
                intervalImprovement="22.26" >
```

He assigns another UI Developer to your team, and lets you borrow a graphic designer from another team who is ramping down on another project.

Note

I've been around a few projects that underwent scrutiny for being late. The upper-management reflex was to offer and add developers, but it rarely works. The ability to show that just adding developers without increasing the capacity surrounding them is a waste of time is invaluable.

Act 8 - Impact (Sensitivity) Analysis

You want to see what most impacts the delivery date; is it the defects or the blocking events? Your graphics designer is complaining about the business being slow to respond to questions. You want to see if that would impact your delivery date by a meaningful amount. You perform a sensitivity analysis on the SimML model.

A sensitivity report gives you an ordered list of what input factors of the model change the delivery date the most. When managing a project it's good to know what factors to go-after and solve next, and a sensitivity reports makes your next opportunity clear. Listing 2-5 shows how to perform a sensitivity simulation.

Listing 2-5

SimML command to execute a sensitivity report. Returns an ordered list of what most influences the output.

```
<sensitivity cycles="250" sortOrder="descending"
estimateMultiplier="0.5" occurenceMultiplier="2"  />
```

The sensitivity analysis is enlightening (Table 2-4) for the development team. It shows that even if the occurrence rate for the specification questions was halved, it would make less than a single day difference to the final outcome. UI Defects remains the highest impacting defect. The development team stops complaining about the lack of response to questions and you get to re-iterate the importance of limiting the UI Defect occurrence rate.

Table 2-4
The results from executing a sensitivity analysis on the model

	UI Defect	Spec question (awaiting answer)	Spec question (awaiting answer)	Block testing (environment down)	Block testing (environment down)	Server-Side Defect
Object Type	Defect	BlockingEvent	BlockingEvent	BlockingEvent	BlockingEvent	Defect
Change Type	Occurence	Estimate	Occurrence	Estimate	Occurence	Occurence
Interval Delta	-3.344	-0.812	-0.744	-0.468	-0.328	-0.248

Project Retrospective

Although it was tight, the addition of a UI coder, a Graphics Designer and a QA Engineer helped quickly resolve some last minute defects and change of scope that Boris and his team wanted after seeing the completed site. The Must-Have features were delivered before the New Year, in mid-December. The Everything-Else delivery group was completed early in the New Year and the extra features helped raise considerable revenue leading up to and over the Christmas and New Year season.

From your perspective, you felt you always had a clear picture of what needed to be managed, and early indications of issues that might risk delivery date promises. Charlie, your boss was also impressed that for every meeting you came prepared with a list of impacting events (a sensitivity report), and knew what staff additions would have the most impact.

Summary

Although this was just a fictional scenario (or was it?) you can quickly see how the use of a model and simulation tools can quickly give you the ability to understand impact of various what-if questions, and the confidence to ask for what you need.

Chapter 3
Introduction to Statistics and Random Number Generation

This book requires a basic level of mathematical ability. When modeling IT projects, we rarely get beyond the basic mathematical operators of plus, minus, multiply and divide – but we do need to understand the terminology of how large groups of numbers are summarized and investigated, a field called Statistics.

The first part of this chapter introduces the statistical terms you need to understand the model and interpret the results of simulations performed later in this book. The second part discusses the intricacies of random number generation. Random numbers play a pivotal role when modeling a process. Random numbers are used as inputs to a model in order to simulate a result, and how these random number inputs are produced and the patterns used can make a model accurately reflect outcomes, or be completely useless.

Statistics 101

Statistics is defined as the mathematics of the collection, organization, and interpretation of numerical data (The Free Dictionary). For the purposes of this book, we use statistics to make sense of the results from a simulation performed over a model of the software development process. Rather than present thousands of numbers, the reports generated for us by the simulation tools described later in this book are summaries of that data using statistical terminology, often called summary statistics. This section refreshes our memory of the mathematical and statistical terms and definitions so that there is no confusion when explaining the examples later in this book.

Summary Statistics

When dealing with large sets of numbers, there are a few important summary statistic measures used to represent different aspects of that set of numbers. We will cover each of these in this section.

Minimum and Maximum

From a large set of numbers, there will be a value that is the lowest value, and a value that will be the highest. There is no limit to the extents that a value is bounded, it will be one of the members of the set of numbers, and if that set has only one member, that minimum and maximum can be the same value. Minimum and maximum has no relationship to zero;

negative numbers will always be less-than the value of any positive number; a minimum value can be, and often is above zero.

Arithmetic Mean (or Standard Average)

The mean value is the sum of all values in a set of numbers, divided by the number of values in that set (Wikipedia). For example, the mean value of the numbers 1, 2, 3, 4, 5 is 3 and calculated as follows –

```
Mean (or standard average)= (1+2+3+4+5) / 5 = 3
```

The mean value is often called the standard average value which is less formal and often more understood by readers of data who don't deal with statistics often. There are other types of averaging algorithms that statistical experts use when dealing with different types of units of measure in elements. The harmonic mean, for example, is a better indicator of average when dealing with ratios and speed or rate (Wikipedia). The geometric mean is a better indicator for exponential growth rates (Wikipedia) where the standard average overstates the growth rate by a small degree. The small errors are rarely an issue with the calculations we employ for software development data, but if you are dealing with life threatening, or large financial decisions – do your own research.

A naming distinction is made to indicate when dealing with a set of data from an entire population (every data-point), or if the data being averaged is a sample from a larger population. When all data is used the mean is referred to as the population mean, when sample data is used, this mean is referred to as a sample mean. This distinction is made to clarify if a value is truly above or below the average value, or if it's just above or below the samples you have taken so far. The more samples added to a set, the closer to the sample mean is to the value of the population mean. It's important that if you have based data or are interpreting results from data that is using a small sample of values, that you differentiate the population versus sample means – consider sample means as an indicator, take a look at the number of samples used (and how they are collected) to make sure that its large enough to trust, and confirm with more samples at the first opportunity.

Median

The median value for a set of number is the value that separates the high half from the low half (Wikipedia). For example, the median for the set of numbers 1, 2, 3, 4, 5 is 3. The process is to order the input set from lowest to highest, and pick the value at the center of the ordered set. If there is an even count of values in the input set, the two numbers at the center of the ordered list are averaged and that number is returned as the median (the mean value). For example, the median for the set of numbers 1, 2, 3, 4, 5, 6 is 3.5 and calculated as follows –

```
Median = (4+3)/2 = 3.5
```

Observing how the median compared to the mode and the mean values is a way to quickly see how skewed the distribution if a set of number might be. The median is less impacted by a few outlier values (those values that are disproportionately higher or lower than most values), and will fall between the mode and the mean values.

For example, for the set of numbers 1, 2, 2, 2, 3, 14, the median value is 2 (as is the mode value), whereas the arithmetic mean value (average) is 4. The single value of 14 made the mean value appear higher, which is correct. When you see the mean and median differ, look closer at the data and confirm for example that the 14 wasn't a data entry mistake by combining a sample of 1 and a sample of 4.

Mode

The mode is the value (or values) in a set of data that occur most frequently (Wikipedia). When more than one value occurs most frequently, meaning they have the same occurrence count, that set of data is said to be multi-modal. The mode will often be different to the mean and the median, especially if the distribution of values in the set of data is offset to one side or the other of the central value. For an input set of numbers 1,2,3,4,4,5 the mode is 4, because 4 occurs twice, and the other numbers once.

Whereas the mean and median require numerical data to compute, the mode can be useful when describing non-numerical data, like the story in a software backlog that has the most defects allocated. When computing the mode with fine-grained numerical data (lots of after the decimal point digits), often no value occurs more than once making the mode an irrelevant measure. In these cases, the data is segmented into ranges, and the mode of the value within those ranges is reported. This serves a similar function as a Histogram (covered shortly).

Standard Deviation

Standard Deviation (σ) is a measure of how close values within a set of numbers are. Conveniently the standard deviation is in the same unit of measure as the numbers being analyzed and is often noted beside the arithmetic mean as an indicator of the likely spread of values around that mean value.

The standard deviation is used to quickly understand what percentage of values fall within a given range of the mean (average) value if that data follows a Normal Distribution. Figure 3-1 graphically shows the percentage of values that fall symmetrically within one, two and three standard deviation values from the mean.

Figure 3-1
Normal Distribution showing Standard Deviation values from mean (Mwtoews, 2007)

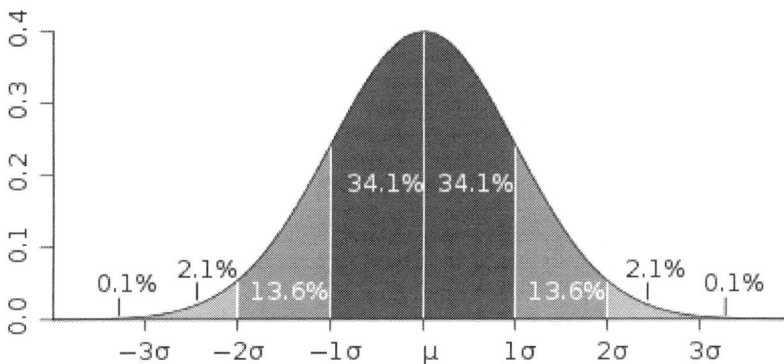

Table 3-1 is a handy quick reference table showing the percentage of values inside and outside listed standard deviation values. For example, at 3 standard deviations either side of the mean value contains 99.7% of all samples.

Table 3-1

Percentage of values within and outside a given number of Standard Deviation values (Wikipedia)

Zσ	Percentage within CI	Percentage outside CI
1σ	68.2689492%	31.7310508%
1.960σ	95%	5%
2σ	95.4499736%	4.5500264%
2.576σ	99%	1%
3σ	99.7300204%	0.2699796%
4σ	99.993666%	0.006334%
5σ	99.9999426697%	0.0000573303%
6σ	99.9999998027%	0.0000001973%
7σ	99.9999999997440%	0.0000000002560%

As with the mean (standard average) value, there is a distinction between the standard deviation of an entire population of data, versus the standard deviation of a subset of data (sample) taken from an entire population. This difference is very small for larger sets of data; with the only calculation difference being a small correction applied to the sample standard deviation where rather than the number of elements in the set used when calculating variance or standard deviation, the number of elements minus one is used (called Bessel's Correction (Wikipedia)). For the most part, the difference is below the threshold that would cause major mathematical errors, but just in case, both are calculated as results from simulations, and called out specifically by name: Population Standard Deviation and Sample Standard Deviation.

Percentile

Percentile is a measure of what percentage of elements (how many out of 100) are likely to fall within a range. 100th percentile is every element, 90th percentile is 9 out of every 10 (or 90 out of every 100) samples taken. Percentile can be quickly estimated using the Standard Deviation and the mean measurements and the percentages shown in Table 3-1.

Table 3-1 is a handy quick reference table showing the percentage of values inside and outside of listed standard deviation values. For example, at 3 standard deviations either side of the mean value, 99.7% of all samples will be accounted for. The 95th percentile for a mean value and a standard deviation can be found using the calculations –

```
95% Low bound = mean - (1.96 x standard deviation)

95% High bound = mean + (1.96 x standard deviation)
```

Percentiles are closely related to Confidence Intervals, where the expectation is set that if you were to take one-hundred samples, a given number of samples would be expected to fall within that range. When estimating, asking for a low and high bound asking for the 90th percentile confidence interval is very common, as it excludes outlier data from the ranges – 5% can be below and 5% can be above that range. This estimation practice is covered in more detail later in this chapter in the section Managing Estimation.

Histograms

Histograms are bar graphs that show the frequency of occurrence of values. When the number of different values gets too large in number, ranges of values are used instead to make the graph manageable to read. Figure 3-2 shows a sample Histogram generated from a simulation model run using Focused Objective's engine. It shows the number of simulation runs that finished for each given number of intervals. For example, the chart shows that 16 simulation runs (read from the vertical axis) completed in 144 intervals (read from the horizontal axis).

Figure 3-2

Sample Histogram. The X-axis is the element value measured; the Y-axis is the occurrence count of elements with that value

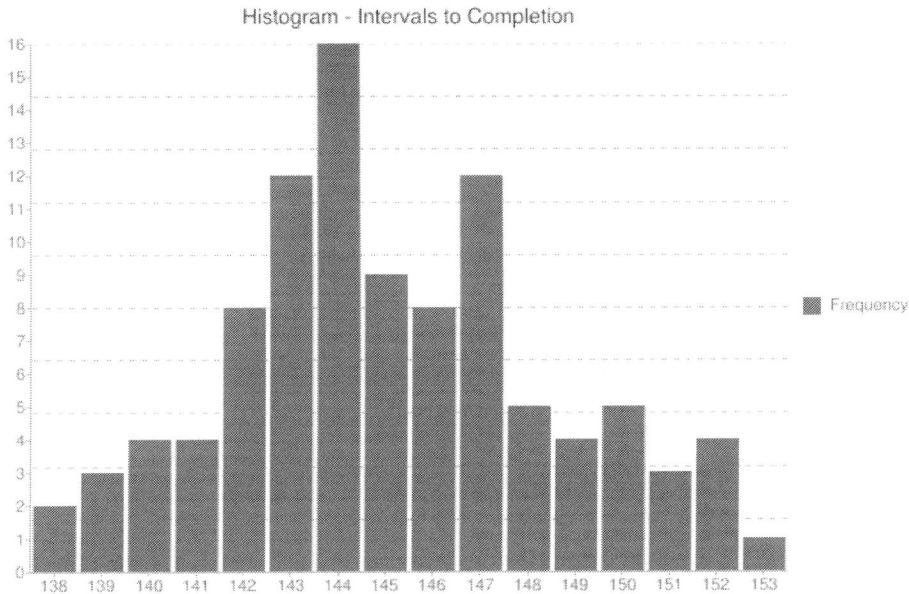

Histograms are a quick way to see the distribution pattern from a set of numerical results. For relatively small sets of numbers, the pattern might be hard to spot, but as more and more samples are plotted, the more likely the pattern for a Normal Distribution curve will emerge (we cover this later under the topic Central Limit Theorem).

Interpreting Simulation Results Summary Statistics

Having defined the various statistical terms used in summarizing a set of result numbers, we will now look at how these values are represented in reports generated by the simulation engine.

Simulation XML Reports

Focused Objective's simulation engine generates XML file reports to capture as much data as possible in a form that is easy for other software to integrate, and for the skilled human to interpret by hand (other reports present a more visually pleasing summary, and we cover those soon).

Statistics are summarized in an element name that describes the measurement be analyzed. Output 3-1 for example, shows the summary statistics for interval measurements generated during a simulation. The outer XML tag, `<statistics>` is the parent to all measures generated in the simulation, and for this example we are showing one of many. The intervals opening tag (`<intervals`) has a number of attributes whose names indicate their measure, and these names have been described earlier in this chapter.

Output 3-1

Sample report output in XML form showing summary statistics for Interval measurements (in this case)

```
<statistics>
  <intervals count="100"  minimum="137" maximum="153"
average="145.25" median="146" mode="147"
populationStandardDeviation="3.128" sampleStandardDeviation="3.144"
fifthPercentile="140" twentyFifthPercentile="143"
seventyFifthPercentile="148" ninetyFifthPercentile="150">
    <histogram>
      <group bin="1" value="137" count="1" />
      <group bin="2" value="139" count="1" />
  [similar to above and below. removed for brevity]
      <group bin="14" value="151" count="1" />
      <group bin="15" value="153" count="1" />

<chart><![CDATA[http://chart.apis.google.com/chart?chxr=0,0,14|1,13
7,153&chxt=y,x&chds=0,14&chbh=a&chs=600x400&cht=bvg&chco=3072F3&chd
=t:1,1,4,7,9,10,11,8,8,14,11,8,6,1,1&chdl=Frequency&chg=0,10&chtt=H
istogram]]></chart>
    </histogram>
  </intervals>
```

Table 3-2 describes each attribute provided in more detail.

Table 3-2
Description of the summary statistic attributes.

Attribute name	Description
count	The number of elements in the dataset being summarized. This is useful to understand if the number of samples is large enough to make conclusions upon (we discuss the Law of Large Numbers and the central limit theorem in the following section)
minimum	The smallest value in the dataset
average	The Arithmetic Mean value or Standard Average of the dataset
maximum	The largest value in the dataset
populationStandard-Deviation	The population standard deviation (standard deviation calculation without Bessel's Correction). All datasets summarized are full populations of results, making this the standard deviation value to use in these reports.
sampleStandard-Deviation	The sample standard deviation that is corrected using the Bessel's Correction (see Standard Deviation for a full description). This is provided in case some future reports employ a sampling approach to data analysis.
median	The median value. For datasets with an odd number of elements, this will be the

	element that is at the 50th percentile of an ordered dataset. If the dataset has an even number of elements, this will be the standard average of the two elements bounding the 50th percentile.
mode	The most common value in the dataset; or a list of up to five of the most common values comma separated; or a list of the most common ranges of values in the format: {greater than value} to {less than or equal-to value}.
fifthPercentile	The calculated 5th percentile. This means that for a dataset following a Normal Distribution, 5% of values would be below this value.
twentyFifthPercentile	The calculated 25th percentile. This means that for a dataset following a Normal Distribution, 25% of values would be below this value.
seventyFifthPercentile	The calculated 75th percentile. This means that for a dataset following a Normal Distribution, 75% of values would be below this value.
ninetyFifthPercentile	The calculated 95th percentile. This means that for a dataset following a Normal Distribution, 95% of values would be below this value.

In addition to the summary statistics for a measure, histogram data is provided to allow the distribution patterns of data to be analyzed. Depending on how many different values are contained in the dataset, slightly different results are generated. These types of results are –

1. Less than twenty different values. The `value` attribute contains the exact value being counted.

```
<histogram>
    <group bin="1" value="8" count="21" />
    <group bin="2" value="9" count="47" />
    <group bin="3" value="10" count="28" />
    <group bin="4" value="11" count="4" />

    <chart><![CDATA[http://chart.apis.google.com/chart?chxr=0,0,4
7|1,8,11&chxt=y,x&chds=0,47&chbh=a&chs=600x400&cht=bvg&chco=3
072F3&chd=t:21,47,28,4&chdl=Frequency&chg=0,10&chtt=Histogram
]]></chart>
</histogram>
```

2. More than twenty different values. Rather than an exact value, the `upToAndIncluding` attribute holds the value that this bin's count is up to and inclusive of. The lower value of the range will be greater than the previous bin's `upToAndIncluding` value, or the minimum value if this is the first bin.

```
<histogram>
    <group bin="1" upToAndIncluding="36.0888" count="2" />
    <group bin="2" upToAndIncluding="36.4486" count="2" />
    [similar to above and below. removed for brevity]
    <group bin="19" upToAndIncluding="42.5652" count="4" />
    <group bin="20" upToAndIncluding="42.925" count="4" />
<chart><![CDATA[http://chart.apis.google.com/chart?chxr=0,0,3
1|1,36.0888,42.925&chxt=y,x&chds=0,31&chbh=a&chs=600x400&cht=
bvg&chco=3072F3&chd=t:2,2,8,7,15,11,14,12,10,31,25,24,20,19,1
8,9,8,7,4,4&chdl=Frequency&chg=0,10&chtt=Histogram]]></chart>
</histogram>
```

Each histogram also has a `<chart>` element which provides a URL to Google's Charting API. These charts are for seeing a simple bar chart representation of the histogram data. An example can be seen in Figure 3-1. To use these, copy and paste the contents of the tag, without the `<![CDATA[` prefix and without the `]]` suffix to the address bar of the web browser application of your choice. A graphics file is produced showing the histogram data as a bar graph.

Generating Random Numbers

Random numbers within a planned range are used in-place of model inputs when simulating real world events that are yet to occur. When planning the input range estimates for simulation models, it is important to have an understanding of different number distributions. In nature and the real world, groups of numbers often follow a pattern. For example, the eye color of people, or the height of people in a region will have a most common value (or range of values) and others that fall above and below that most common. This type of number distribution is called a Normal Distribution and it is one of many that are possible. Understanding number distributions and how random numbers can be generated with specific characteristics to match the real world likelihood is an important skill to improve the accuracy of any model and simulation.

Random Number Generators

Computers don't do random well, in fact they don't do random at all. A step by step algorithm that a computer can use to generate statistical random (pseudo-random) sets of numbers is the best we can achieve, and this is defined as - "a numeric sequence is said to be statistically random when it contains no recognizable patterns or regularities" (Wikipedia).

There are many algorithms used for generating random numbers that satisfy the statistical random definition, but it is important to make sure that the one you are using does. At a minimum, before trusting a random number generator, produce a set of results and produce a histogram chart. It should follow a uniform distribution pattern (covered next). If absolutely ensuring that the data is random is important to you, generating a set of numbers and applying the Diehard Battery of Tests for Randomness (Marsaglia, 1995) found online at http://www.stat.fsu.edu/pub/diehard/ over the data. It's rare you need to do this, and the random number generators used in Focused Objective's simulation tools are statistically random.

When generating random numbers, the distribution pattern, meaning what frequency values in a certain range occur is of key concern. We will now cover the basic distribution patterns, giving you enough background to model effectively.

Uniform Distribution

A uniform distribution is where every value between a given range has an equal likelihood as another. Tossing an unmodified coin for instance, yields an equal likelihood of heads versus tails. Rolling a six-sided die has an equal likelihood of yielding a 1, 2, 3, 4, 5 or 6 for each roll, and no-matter how many individual rolls are performed, no individual result will become more common. Figure 3-3 simulates rolling a dice 5,000 times using the Excel function =RANDBETWEEN(1,6) and then plotting the results as a histogram. You will note that not all bins have exactly the same frequency, but as more samples are calculated, the closer they will become. This follows the Law of Large Numbers theory that states the more samples, the closer to the calculated probability (and mean value) the results will be.

Figure 3-3

Histogram of 5,000 uniform distribution values between 1 and 6 (simulating a common dice roll)

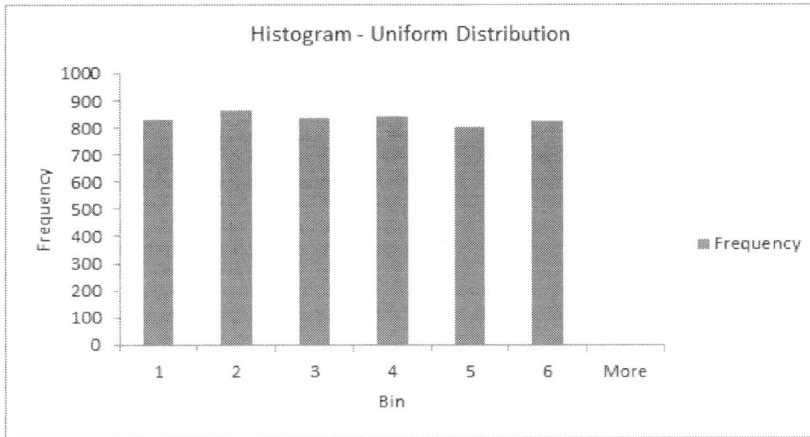

When creating a model, it is initially good practice to use a uniform distribution between the lower and upper 95% estimated Confidence Intervals, unless you are certain another number distribution pattern is in effect. This is the default number distribution used in Focused Objective's simulation engine unless otherwise configured.

Normal Distribution (AKA Bell Curve) and the Central Limit Theorem

The Normal Distribution or the Bell Curve is the best known number distribution pattern, and its classic shape can be seen in Figure 3-4. The Normal Distribution seems to be a number distribution shape often found in nature and in many commercial situations. It prevalence is due to the Central Limit Theorem, which simply states – "the mean of a sufficiently large number of independent random variables, each with finite mean and variance, will be approximately normally distributed" (Wikipedia).

Figure 3-4

Probability distribution chart for a Normal function. Y-Axis is frequency, X-Axis is the value. This picture is a histogram shown as a line graph rather than a bar graph.

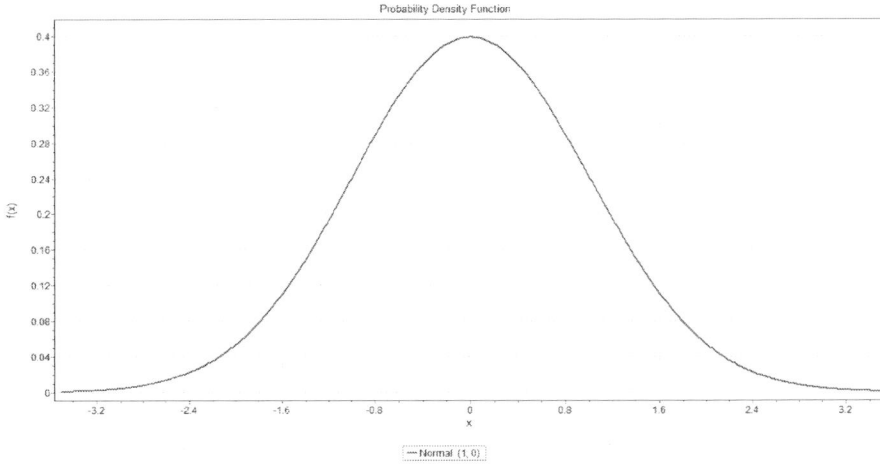

One way of explaining this is to sum the total story points for 5 user stories that are estimated to take from 1 story point to 5 story points. If we generate random numbers for each stories story points (uniform random numbers, no pattern, each value 1 to 5 has equal likelihood), and sum these 5,000 times, we get what is approximately a Normal Distribution as shown in Figure 3-5. Whilst not a perfect Normal Distribution, the Central Limit Theorem says that we would get closer to a Normal Distribution the more samples we measured.

Figure 3-5

Histogram from the results of 5,000 samples: Sum of 5 random (uniform) values of 1 to 5

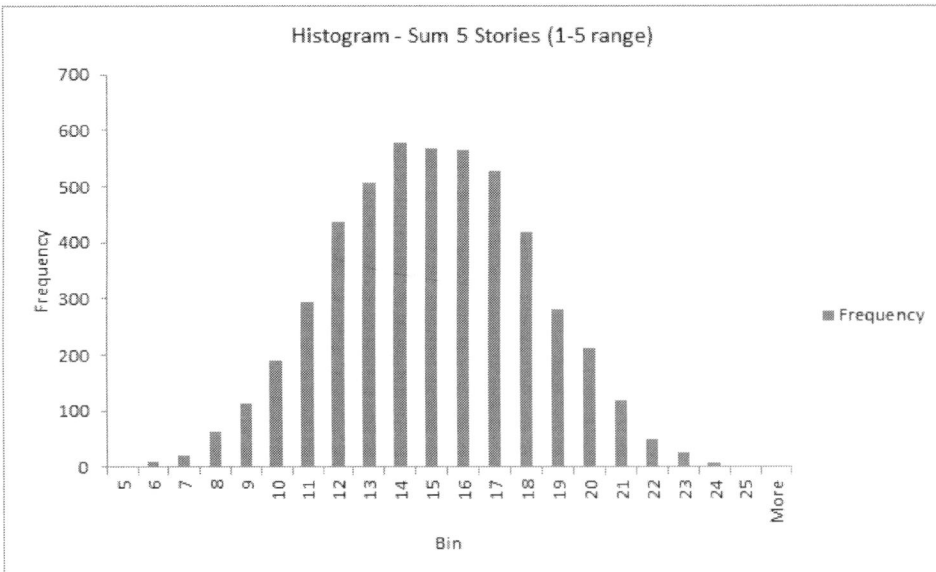

When creating models for software development and IT portfolios, the summing nature of the models, with defined uncertainty (estimate ranges) means our results are often Normally Distributed. We are often dealing with small sets of data, and the histograms may look less refined than that shown in Figure 3-5, but the Central Limit Theorem says that the more samples, the more Normal the results will become. To confirm this, I often artificially increase the sample size just to confirm that the final histogram results do become normal. By knowing this, we can start to make predictions about what the mean, standard deviation and 95th percentiles will be with very few samples, as low as 15-25 in number.

Not everybody is a fan of the Normal Distribution for forecasting the future, Nassim Taleb in the entertaining and educational book, The Black Swan: The Impact of the Highly Improbable (Taleb, 2007) labels the Bell Curve an "Intellectual Fraud," noting its weakness in the presence of high magnitude outliers, and mentions that "half of the return of the stock market over the past fifty years was associated with just ten days with the greatest daily change." Taleb though admits that the Bell Curve works well when dealing with variables that don't deviate much from the mean value, and for the most part, we should heed his warnings to be vigilant in digging deeper into data presented. To help avoid errors, we never remove outliers from data presented in results, and always show histogram data whenever a mean (standard average) and standard deviation value is presented. Always confirm the histogram is a close approximation of a histogram without major outlier values before believing the standard deviation, percentiles, mean or median.

When the results of a histogram doesn't follow the normal distribution shape, and is offset in some way left or right of the mean value, this is called a Skewed Distribution.

Skewed Distributions

Skewed distribution patterns are when the frequency of some values is higher at the lower or the upper end of a range. This isn't an unlikely pattern for the time taken to complete software development tasks and stories. It's not uncommon for well planned projects to follow a Lognormal pattern of distribution with more story estimates being at the lower end, with larger stories declining rapidly in frequency. Figure 3-6 shows one such probability distribution curve that might apply, lots of size 1 and 2 story points, declining over 3, 4, 5 and 6 story point estimates with a few larger (too big?) stories.

There are hundreds of distribution functions documented, but about twenty five are the most commonly used. Each distribution function helps our model create random numbers that fall in line with real-world likelihood. In Chapter 11 we take a detailed look at how to examine prior data and determine what distribution pattern will improve the accuracy of our model.

How to use custom distribution patterns for simulation is an advanced topic and not directly covered in this book (see FocusedObjective.com for articles and reference on building and using custom distributions). Using the development events, blocking events and added scope as listed in Chapter 6, and by splitting the backlog as covered in Chapter 5, we do create distributions in our model. The benefit of building distributions using these events is the ability to perform sensitivity analysis and find what event is most impacting delivery forecast.

Figure 3-6

Probability distribution chart for a Lognormal function. Y-Axis is frequency, X-Axis is the value.

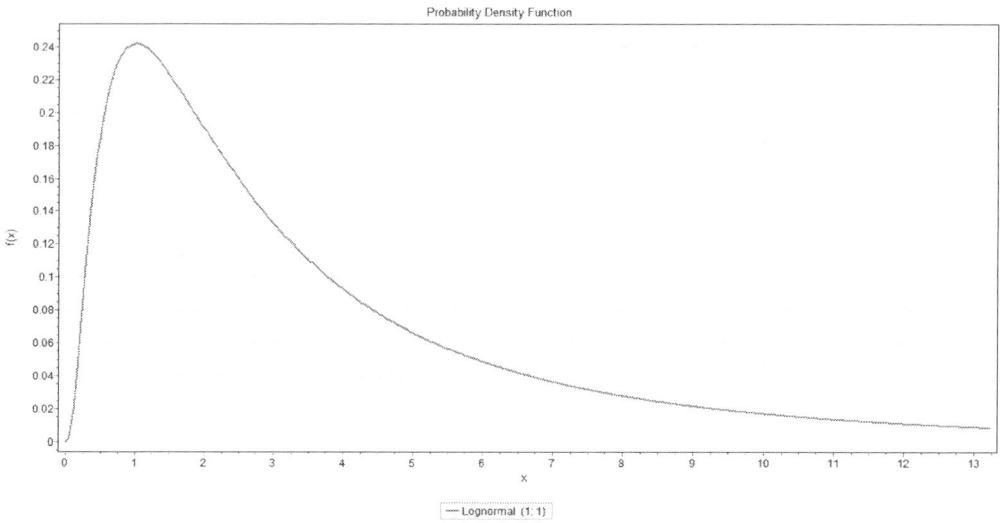

Probability Density Function

Lognormal (1; 1)

Figure 3-7

Just a few continuous distribution functions to generate random numbers that follow specific patterns

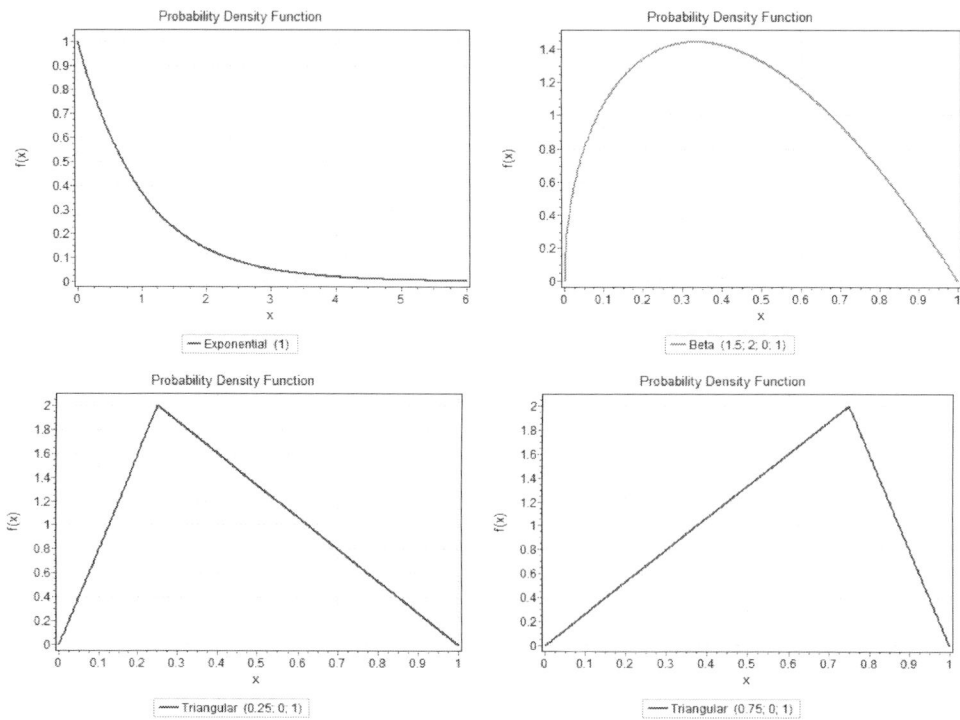

Probability Density Function

Exponential (1)

Probability Density Function

Beta (1.5; 2; 0; 1)

Probability Density Function

Triangular (0.25; 0; 1)

Probability Density Function

Triangular (0.75; 0; 1)

Summary

This chapter has outlined the statistical terms and background required to model effectively. Entire books are devoted to each of the topics in this chapter, and the more you learn about statistics and random-numbers, the better you will be able to produce and interpret simulation model results – consider investing in a good statistic book to gain more knowledge on this subject.

The next chapter applies the concept of 95th Percent Confident Interval's for obtaining expert opinion estimates on inputs to our models, and important first step in reliable model simulation.

Chapter 4
Just Enough Estimation

In Chapter 1 we introduced the concepts and relationship between estimation and forecasting. To simulate a model and produce a forecast date or cost, inputs to a model need to be estimated. The process we describe and use throughout this book estimates ranges and number distribution patterns rather than exact values. This allows the simulation model to find a range of viable solutions in which to analyze. The techniques in this book reduce time and quantity of estimates needed, but to model, forecast and manage risk; we still need some data to evaluate.

Estimation Art

Software development often works at or outside near the edge of innovation, at least for the individuals tasked with turning a vision into reality, and although in most cases software development isn't life threatening, the words of Richard Feynman in a report on the failure of adequately managing risk in the Space Shuttle program -

"The Space Shuttle Main Engine is a very remarkable machine. It has a greater ratio of thrust to weight than any previous engine. It is built at the edge of, or outside of, previous engineering experience. Therefore, as expected, many different kinds of flaws and difficulties have turned up." (Feynman, 1986)

When we are asked to estimate software projects, we request people to estimate at the edge of their experience, often beyond prior art. Therefore we have to rely on our experience combined with a good dose of imagination as to what flaws and difficulties will turn up. Don't under-estimate (oops, no pun intended) just how hard it is to get software development estimates close – which is why we need to manage the risks so effectively, and why the techniques in this book are proposed.

To perform modeling and simulation, estimates take the following form –

1. 90th percentile range estimate "tell me the lowest and highest likely value?"
2. The likely distribution of estimates "would you expect equal likelihood over the range, or more weighted towards one end?"
3. Correlation to other estimates "Would other factors estimated influence this factor? What would that relationship be?"

Not all the estimates require the three pieces of detail, and for first pass simulation, only the 90th percentile range is necessary. This chapter discusses how to train, facilitate and obtain the required information from experts to get accurate 90th percentile ranges.

Estimating the 90th Percentile Range

When obtaining opinion from experts about the likely range of values for an input variable of a model, it is easier for those experts (you in this case) to think in ranges rather than exact values.

Tying people down to an estimate is difficult enough, but the more someone knows about a problem, the more their mind swerves to-and-fro thinking about all the things that can go wrong. The more you know, the more you have experienced outliers; that once or twice in one-hundred sample event that still haunts you too this day – better double my estimate a few times. Meet the "over-estimator" personality (rare, but not extinct). The flip-side to thinking about all of the things that can go wrong, are the people who assume that any task will go perfectly, and that their role is the only role to play in order to deliver a feature or product. Meet the "chronic under-estimator" personality (often in plague proportions around IT projects).

The under-estimation personality type is in abundance, the over-estimator less-so, but both types of estimation error cause terrible software forecast results. To achieve any chance of accuracy, you need to take input from both sets of people, and the range of possible values need to reflect both confidence types. But, not the extremes – allowing estimate ranges to reflect the events with less than a 5% chance can widen ranges to an unusable level and skew results wildly high or low as estimates are simulated (or worse just totaled up).

Asking expert opinion to provide a 90th percentile range estimate (what would be called a Confidence Interval if we had actual samples to plot, it's probably correct to call this a Confidence Interval unless there is a statistician ion your team) rather than obsessing over an exact value can help facilitate meaningful discussion about where risk truly lay and how likely those risks are to occur. As a short refresher, in Chapter 3 we defined a 90th percentile confidence interval as meaning that 90 percent of samples would fall within the range given, 5 percent above and 5 percent below the range. The range would be from the 5th percentile to the 95th percentile of the dataset in question.

After deciding you need an estimate for a model, and have exhausted all ways of grouping and estimating at a higher level (See Reducing the Amount of Estimation later in this chapter), it's time to grab a subject matter expert(s) and get them to put their experience into the form of an estimate.

Coaching Experts on 90th Percentile Estimation

Different people have different biases because of their experience; no two individuals have the same work history and day to day experience, so it is little wonder each person will apply different "expert opinion" judgment to an estimate.

It takes practice to become familiar and competent in estimating a 90th percent range. In his book The Failure of Risk Management and how to fix it, Douglas Hubbard (Hubbard, 2009) describes techniques to help calibrate experts into giving superior 90th percentile range estimates. His techniques take would-be estimators through practice questions in order to help them understand how over-confident they are, even when they are wrong! Starting each estimation session by asking the assembled experts to determine the 90th percentile range of a question where the answer can be immediately disclosed is a great way to re-enforce the goal. You get to coach the assembled that it's not a competition to find an exact estimate, it's a competition to make sure that they are confident the final actual result is somewhere in the range they choose nine out of ten times. The training questions in Douglas Hubbard's book are simple questions to research (make sure no smart-phones and laptops are open, Wikipedia knows all), but unlikely that anyone in the room knows the answer already. Some examples are: "What is the height of the Statue of Liberty?" and "What was the population of China in 2000?" Your goal is to help the experts improve their mental process for finding the lowest they think possible, and the highest they think possible, and the all-important – why.

At first, many experts choose a narrow range, almost trying to impress the facilitator as to how small a range they can guess. Hubbard (Hubbard, 2009), offers some strategies on how to get the expert to understand their certainty better. His advice (and others quoted in his book), suggests that humans get very well attuned to risk when money is involved. Offering someone even a hypothetical chance to win or lose cash tunes their risk radar that little bit more. His technique gives the expert a choice, one that is absolutely a 9 out of 10 chance of winning, and then the asks them whether they prefer their chances on their estimate choice, or the fixed choice. Following a similar concept, here is a hypothetical conversation that uses this method -

You: "How long do you think it will take to test each of the new booking pages? There are five of them, but let's just focus on how long to test one of them."

Expert: "One hour."

You: "OK, but we are after a low-bound and high-bound number here, a range that you would be confident, 90% confident to hit."

Expert: "One to three hours."

You: "Alright, remember we are looking for a range that would be 90% certain of hitting, missing one time in ten stories. Let me make it interesting to explore how confident you are in your range, What if I offered you a choice –

Option A. You will win $1,000 if your colleagues agree and their ranges turn out to be similar to yours or narrower than the numbers you gave for the upper and lower bounds. If not, you win nothing.

Option B. You draw a marble at random from a bag of nine green marbles and one red marble. If the marble is green, you win $1,000. If it is red, you win nothing (i.e., there is a 90% chance you win $1,000).

About now, you will see if the expert truly trusts their range, and most often they won't – they are probably somewhat certain, but not 90% just yet. It seems so obvious that the bag of marbles has a much greater chance of being true, and that would only be true if they had some misgivings about their range.

Expert: "I might be a bit narrow of the high side. Considering these pages have a lot more dynamic code, and we need to test multiple browsers, in hindsight, I'd like to increase both ranges. Low bound of 6 hours and high-bound of 12 hours."

This type of technique is called an Equivalence Bet, or the Equivalence Urn method for subjective risk determination. It works because human intuition grasps the concept that drawing the marbles from a container (urn) has an equal probability for every marble. It's easy for the brain to compute the likelihood of getting odd-color-out marble. Less so than their estimate, but the mental process of equating something absolutely 90% versus their estimate should help widen the range to acceptable – or at least test how confident they are in their peers.

It's important to remember that when building a model starting with wide ranges that you are certain the real-world likely value falls between is most paramount. Later in this book we cover how to ascertain what factors and estimates are causing the most impact, and those factors should be the first you revisit and ask more questions about in order to narrow the estimate range with considered discussion. At the moment you might just be wasting time in narrowing an estimate that doesn't impact the results (a forecast of date or cost) in a meaningful way. Avoid premature narrowing of estimates, and encourage your experts to think broadly.

Another important aspect when coaching an expert of giving a 90th percentile range estimate is they often think of the most likely single value estimate and apply their own plus and minus range. The low-bound has a completely different set of factors impacting it's boundaries than the high-bound in an estimate. For example, the low-bound would be the limit of everything going right, and the upper-bound everything with more than a 5% chance going wrong. Other than having to be larger than the low-bound, the high-bound should and will be most impacted by difficulties making a smooth, single pass progress from start to complete. To avoid this type of anchoring estimation problem occurring, consider the following conversation, which extends the previous conversation –

You: "OK. 6 hours low-bound, 12 hours upper-bound. Let's look at them separately for a moment. 6 hours for the low-bound. Can you tell me at least two reasons why you think that is the fastest time you can test one of these pages."

Expert: "It takes at least three hours for me to get the latest build into my test environment, and other hour to define all the test data I might need like fake customer accounts from different countries and regions. And then two hours to manually test."

You: "Good. How often does it take longer than three hours to setup the environment, and how often does it take longer than one hour to create test data. If you think these happen more than 5% of the time, we should consider increasing that boundary."

Expert: "No, its automated now, and I'm happy it fails less often than 5 in 100 times, and when it does its less than an hour to fix."

You: "Great, 6 hours it is. Now let's focus on the upper-bound. Give me a couple of worst case scenarios for testing these new pages."

Expert: "The Javascript and CSS code often fails subtly on different browsers. So, we need to test on each separately. IE 6, 7 and 8, Firefox, and Chrome. IE 6 often is problematic – so I often have to ask the business owner if the degraded functionality is OK. That takes time."

You: "OK, how likely does IE 6 cause issues? And how long for the business owner to OK the degradation?"

Expert : "About 30% of the pages, and at least a day to get the OK."

You: "OK, we can control how often the larger estimate is used later, for now to get the range correct, any event occurring 30% of the time has to be considered for the top boundary. Initially you only increased the upper-bound by 6 hours, shouldn't that be at least a day? How long would it take to test everything, and allow for the day turnaround in answering the degradation question?"

Expert: "OK, I get it. I'm very comfortable with the 6 hours for all other events, but you are right, it could be at least a day more waiting for an answer on the IE6 experience. Let's go with 14 hours, 6 hours to test, and worst case a day of 8 hours waiting for response."

You: "Perfect. And we'll make a note that you expect most times to be around the 6 hour mark, with a 30% chance of being up to the 14 day range."

It's the conversation that matters. You are coaching them to consider events and the likelihood of those events, and you are capturing data that can be used to formulate a distribution pattern within that range. The conversation process takes the following format -

1. Present the low boundary.
2. Ask what factors they used in their thinking to form the lower boundary. Was it setup time, having done similar tasks before, or was it just because they anchored on an average and applied a range (bad habit).
3. Capture the events and likelihood of those events that might increase the lower-bound. We use this when considering distribution patterns. For now, if an event is more likely than 5 times in 100, help them incorporate this event into their low-bound estimate.
4. Present the upper boundary.
5. Capture the events and likelihood of those events that might increase the upper-bound. We use this when considering distribution patterns. For now, if an event is more likely than 5 times in 100, help them incorporate this event into their upper-bound estimate.
6. Remind them that the range should be 90th percentile, and we are yet to decide which parts of the range are more common and less common than any other.

Every conversation will be different, and in most cases you are not the expert, but I find the template shown in Figure 4-1 helps capture the information required. Your job as coach is to make sure the expert understands the goal of a 90th percentile range, and that the right process to exclude the lowest 5% of outliers and the upper 5th percent of outliers are excluded. It is also your job to not get estimates when they may not add value to the model. This is achieved by estimating in groups, which we will cover now.

Figure 4-1

Sample estimation worksheet for coaching experts on finding the low-bound and upper-bound 90th percentile range

Sample Estimation Worksheet Form

Low-bound - Describe any events that need to happen before any work can be performed and what events that could cause this work to take longer? The first row contains an example. (Table 1)

Event/Task Description	Likelihood Percentage	Estimate	Notes
E.g. Setup test environment	80%	4 hours	Automated. Fails rarely < 5%

If there were absolutely no issues, everything went smoothly, how long do you expect the work to take? Describe the tasks and their likely estimate for each task if everything went well. The first row contains an example. (Table 2)

Event/Task Description	Estimate	Notes
E.g. Meet with designer	1 hours	Make sure all of the icons are ready and review CSS

Low-bound = Sum of Table 1 where likelihood percentage > 5% + Sum of Table 2

Upper-Bound - Describe any events that will add work to the steps in Table 2 (the best case scenario). Think carefully about the likelihood value here; you are specifying the percentage likelihood of this event occurring, for example 100% mean certain every time, 50% means every second time, 10% means once every 10 times. The first row contains an example. (Table 3 – Events that cause extra work to occur)

Event/Task Description	Likelihood Percentage	Estimate (95th percentile)	Notes
E.g. Trouble getting IE6 working	75%	4 hours	

Upper-bound = Low-bound + (Sum of estimates in Table 3 where likelihood > 5%)

Reducing the Amount of Estimation to a Minimum

Good estimation takes time; time the experts could be performing actual deliverable work, and getting revenue generating product into the marketplace. In Chapter 1 we covered the benefits of modeling and being able to forecast accurately, but constantly ask yourself when building the model - do I need this estimate? Is this estimate going to dramatically impact the outcome? If the answer is yes, then it is important to consider ways of reducing the effort.

This section examines ways of grouping similar work efforts and estimating them as a single piece of work rather than individually. In addition to saving time, estimating software features like this can often help the team understand the features in more detail and give better estimate accuracy.

The theory here is simple. Find ways of grouping work that is similar in some way, and estimate once for what an individual piece of work in that group. This estimate is then used for all work items in that group. This will quickly get you estimates for a first pass model, and once the model is producing data, it is possible to see the impact of each group. If one group is impacting the model more than the others, you can estimate the work in that group in more detail. The key point is that you don't estimate every work item up-front unless a group is influencing the output to a degree that is impacting a forecast.

There are countless ways of grouping work. I'll cover a few here so you get the idea. The only caveat of creating a group is that each member of the group will share the same estimate boundaries. They will take similar time, or occur at a similar rate.

Grouping by "Size"

This is often the most common grouping. It's often called T-Shirt sizing, or ROM (rough order of magnitude). The result you want is a backlog of work where each item is in one of up to a small number of groups. Possible group sizes can be small, medium, large, extra-large for example, or numerical, 1, 2, 3, 5, 8, 13, 20 or some variant thereof. Once the work is segmented into these groups, you can ask the experts to assign a 90th percentile range for the group (how long it would take to do a single item in the group, not how long to do all work in the group).

The basic idea is you present a work item, you introduce that item (explain what it is), and then ask the group to yell out a size. Unless someone in the group has a strong feeling they disagree with the average size "yelled-out", you move quickly to the next story. If there is wide disparity, you discuss and vote again until consensus is reached.

One practical implementation of this technique is a group card game called Planning Poker (Grenning, 2002). James Grenning proposed using a simple card game technique to avoid estimation paralysis during estimation sessions. His technique asks the experts assembled to quickly make a guess of the estimate size using a set of pre-printed cards. If everybody agrees, that estimate is recorded; if they disagree, then the group discusses (set a time limit so that you don't get too caught up on item) why the differences occurred and comes to consensus. Very quickly the group learns the reasons other experts give a higher or lower opinion, and self-moderates (differences become less extreme, but you want to encourage differences, the discussion is invaluable). Overall this technique is well received by participants, and all experts get an equal voice, rather than just the loudest.

Tip: Planning Poker

When researching this chapter I came across a free online tool that provides planning poker across the Internet: http://planningpoker.com. It's a simple and practical implementation.

Planning Poker is one way of obtaining size estimates from a group of experts. The important factors in any technique are –

1. The work item is introduced by the owner and described so that everybody understands the intention and scope. Single line Excel spreadsheet descriptions are not good enough.

2. Each member of the group gives their opinion on size.

3. The group discusses the disparity and moves to consensus.

4. If a work item is deemed too large to estimate (higher than the highest pre-set estimate value), then the work item is split and estimated as two or more pieces.

5. Set a two or three minute time-box of conversation for reaching consensus or deferring that estimate.

This technique still estimates every work item, but rather than obtain a 90th percentile range for every story, you abbreviate the expert estimation time to once for every group size (as the example shown in Table 4-1), and an quick pass through the backlog to group similarly sized work items with the group of choice.

Table 4-1

Sample estimates by size. Rather than estimate every story, just assign a small, medium, large or extra-large to each story, and estimate these groups once (like this table). For Kanban, a different cycle-time would be used instead of points.

	5th percentile estimate (points)	95th percentile estimate (points)
Small	1	3
Medium	2	5
Large	5	8
Extra-large	8	20

Grouping by "Type"

Different work items in a backlog share common development processes. For example, some work items might be totally database and web-service centric; others might demand very clever UI skills for writing interactive web-pages. If these work items were sorted by size alone, they might end up in the same "medium" bucket, even though they require different experts to work on them.

If you are modeling and forecasting the different staffing levels for certain skills, having a backlog divided by the predominant skillsets required to produce each item is necessary. In this case, modeling different cycle-times for Kanban columns, or under-standing the story size allocation for each skillset member of a team help make important staffing decisions through simulation. Table 4-2 shows an example set of cycle-time estimations for different types of work in a hypothetical backlog for a website. Some columns don't require any work time at all for estimation.

Table 4-2

Sample categorization scheme for website backlog. Different types of work can have different column cycle-times estimates for modeling.

	Kanban Columns Cycle-Time (90th percentile range in days)				
	UI Design	Server-side / DB	UI Develop	Analytics	QA / Test
UI Heavy (First Time) Pages	3 to 5	1 to 3	3 to 8	0 to 0	2 to 5
UI Heavy (Repeat) Pages	1 to 3	1 to 3	1 to 4	0 to 0	1 to 3
Web-service / Database Work	0 to 0	3 to 5	0 to 0	1 to 2 (error logging)	3 to 5
Logging / Business Analytics	0 to 0	1 to 2	1 to 2	2 to 5	1 to 5

Another way to categorize for iteration based agile development system, like Scrum is to divide the total story points in each estimate group by the job skill required. Table 4-3 shows one way of partitioning story points in order model staff utilization when allocating story points.

Table 4-3

Sample categorization scheme for website backlog. Different types of work can have different point estimates by job function for modeling staff utilization in addition to just work-time.

	Scrum Skill Point Allocation (90th percentile range in points)				
	Graphic Designers	Java Server Side Devs	HTML / CSS / JS Devs	Analytics / Data Warehousing	QA / Test
UI Heavy (First Time) Pages	3 to 5	1 to 3	3 to 8	0 to 0	2 to 5
UI Heavy (Repeat) Pages	1 to 3	1 to 3	1 to 4	0 to 0	1 to 3
Web-service / Database Work	0 to 0	3 to 5	0 to 0	1 to 2 (error logging)	3 to 5
Logging / Business Analytics	0 to 0	1 to 2	1 to 2	2 to 5	1 to 5

Every project will have different type categorizations. The main point is a different allocation of cycle-time or story-points can be allocated in a meaningful way for the model being created. If additional finer-grain detail is required, this categorization can be combined with grouping by size, in which case a small, medium and large (for example) option for each of these group by type options.

Summary

This chapter has discussed how to quickly and reliably obtain a 90th percentile range estimate from experts, and how to reduce the time taken to get those experts to reach agreement. Every effort should be to reduce the amount of estimation required, but as every project is different, somebody needs to ascertain what work needs to be done, and how long that work may take to complete.

Chapter 5
Simulation Modeling Language Basics

This chapter introduces the basic structure and format of the Simulation Modeling Language (or SimML pronounced 'sim-el'). This is a custom language that allows software projects and project structures to be captured in a single text file for simulation. By the end of this chapter you will have a better understanding of how to describe a backlog of project work, and how to setup Kanban and Scrum project simulations. This chapter only covers the mandatory elements of a SimML file; following chapters cover the optional events that build upon these basics to improve accuracy.

Simulation Modeling Language – SimML

SimML is a simple custom language for modeling software projects and processes, allowing models to be quickly built and refined over time. The file format is a simple text file conforming to the rules in the W3C XML File specification (Bray, Paoli, Sperberg-McQueen, Maler, & Yergeau, 2008). This standard describes XML files in detail, but in essence, an XML file is a text file format where the text data is nestled between sets of open (e.g. `<simulation>`) and closing (e.g. `</simulation>`) tags. Values can be specified between the tags, or as attributes within the opening tag for example –

```
<simulation name="value as attribute in opening tag here">
      value between tag here
</simulation>
```

Sections in an XML file can also have sub-sections. This is where an opening and closing XML tag is within the opening and closing tag of another section. There is no limit to this nesting structure, and SimML uses this technique to four levels in some cases.

A SimML specific XML file consists of three sections (the name of the tag), which will be covered in detail throughout this and the next few chapters –

1. *Simulation*: the root element for the file format.
2. *Setup*: for defining the team, project and events to model.
3. *Execute*: for defining the types of simulation to execute and report.

Simulation Section

The simulation section of a SimML file contains the one root tag element `simulation`, which then contains the sub elements: `setup` and `execute` as defined further in this chapter. Listing 5-1 shows the basic structure of a SimML file.

The `simulation` element has one mandatory attribute, `name`, which is a user defined name for the simulation file. This name is used for matching result files and for user future reference when examining this file, but can be anything as long as doesn't contain an opening or closing angle bracket (less-than or greater than sign).

Listing 5-1

A SimML file has a simulation element at the root of the document and an execute and setup section within its opening and closing element tags.

```
<simulation name="Simple SimML File">
  <execute>
  </execute>
  <setup>
  </setup>
</simulation>
```

Execute section

The execute section of a SimML file contains instructions to the simulation engine, telling it what analysis you wish carried out. The execute section contains no information relating to the project or the process being undertaken, it just gives execution instructions to the simulation engine and controls how the results will be formatted.

Each execute sub-section carries out a different simulation task covered in Chapters 7 to 11. In this chapter we cover the project model section of the SimML file – the `setup` section.

Setup Section

The setup section of a SimML file contains the model to be simulated. There are many valid sub-elements that can be used to describe a software project and process. Different ones will be required depending on if you are simulating an iterative story point methodology (like Scrum) or a cycle-time column based process (like Lean or Kanban). New sections are added as new simulation features become available over time, at the time of writing, the following setup sections are available –

- *Added Scope*: Definition of one or more scope creep events (refactoring, new stories, etc.)
- *Backlog*: Definition and partitioning of the work to be completed.
- *Blocking Events*: Definition of one or more blocking events (awaiting information, etc.).
- *Columns*: Definition of status columns for Lean/Cycle-Time methodologies.

- *Defects*: Definition of one or more defect occurrences (bugs, re-work, etc.).
- *Iteration*: Definition of iteration details for Iterative/Story Point based methodologies.

Each section has many attributes of its own. Later in this chapter we cover the essential sections: Backlog, Columns and Iteration. In upcoming chapters, we will examine the optional Added Scope, Blocking Events and Defects sections.

Example SimML Files

SimML files grow in complexity as models expand in detail. Listing 5-2 shows the simplest SimML file for executing a visual simulation of an iteration based project of 30 various sized stories. The attribute names for the most part are descriptive enough to understand their intention and every aspect of these files will be elaborated upon in this and upcoming chapters. Figure 5-1 shows the Scrum Board Viewer that is launched when this SimML file is executed using Focused Objective's Simulation Engine. For the moment though, consider this the "Hello World" of SimML files (printing Hello World to the screen is the first demo used when showing a new computer language).

Listing 5-2

Simple Agile Scrum SimML file example.

```
<simulation name="Scrum simple file"  >

   <execute type="scrum">
      <visual />
   </execute>

   <setup>
      <iteration storyPointsPerIterationLowBound="10"
              storyPointsPerIterationHighBound="15" />

      <backlog type="custom">
         <custom name="Small" count="10"
                 estimateLowBound="1" estimateHighBound="3" />
         <custom name="Medium" count="10"
                 estimateLowBound="3" estimateHighBound="6" />
         <custom name="Large" count="10"
                 estimateLowBound="6" estimateHighBound="10" />
      </backlog>
   </setup>
</simulation>
```

Figure 5-1

Scrum Board Viewer launched when executing the SimML file shown in Listing 5-2.

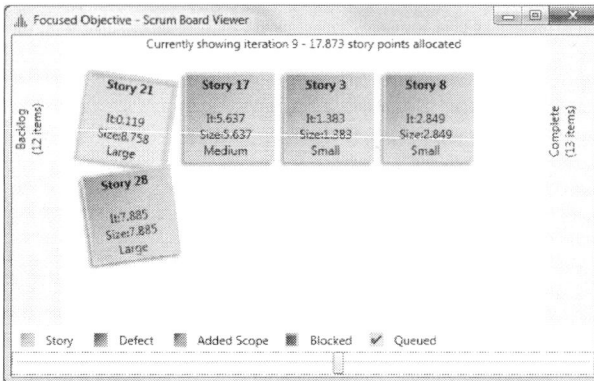

Kanban simulation is just as straightforward Listing 5-3 shows a simple SimML file that produces the visual simulation of a Kanban status board as shown in Figure 5-2. In this model, the Kanban board has 3 columns, and the simulation moves 30 cards from the backlog to complete over time.

Listing 5-3

Simple Lean/Kanban SimML file.

```
<simulation name="Kanban simple file"  >
  <execute type="kanban">
    <visual />
  </execute>
  <setup>

    <backlog type="simple" simpleCount="30" />

    <columns>
       <column id="1" estimateLowBound="1" estimateHighBound="2"
                  wipLimit="1">
          Design
       </column>
       <column id="2" estimateLowBound="1" estimateHighBound="5"
                  wipLimit="4">
          Develop
       </column>
       <column id="3" estimateLowBound="1" estimateHighBound="2"
                  wipLimit="2">
          Test
       </column>
    </columns>

  </setup>
</simulation>
```

Figure 5-2
Kanban Board Viewer launched when executing the SimML file shown in Listing 5-3.

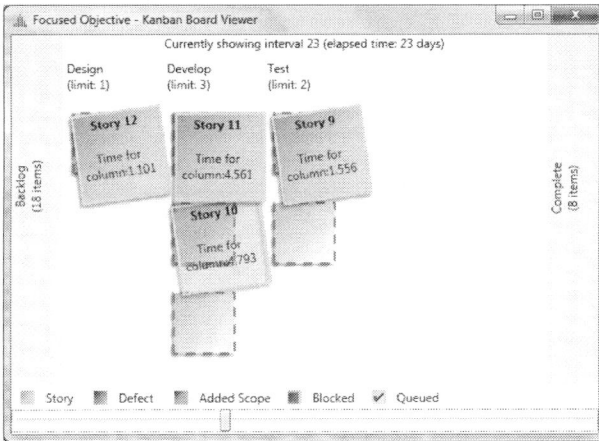

These simple SimML examples are just to show you the basic mechanics of a SimML file. You have seen the basic structure of both types of development methodologies supported: Lean/Kanban and Agile/Scrum. We will now cover the SimML differences when modeling each methodology type.

Lean/Kanban Modeling versus Agile/Scrum Modeling

SimML support both iterative styles of agile development where work is delivered at regular defined intervals and a team targets a specific amount of work in that time, and Lean styles of agile development where a team moves work through a series of steps (status columns) in a target period of time (called cycle-time). You need to pick the one that most closely matches your development methodology before modeling, because the choice does impose restrictions in the form of validation rules when testing and executing simulations on your model. The biggest differences are noted in Table 5-1, and most involve the choice of either story-points or cycle-time estimation.

Table 5-1
Differences in SimML definitions for Scrum and Kanban methodologies.

Feature	Agile/Scrum (iterative, points)	Lean/Kanban (columns, cycle-times)
Estimates	Story points (in whatever unit you choose)	Simulation Intervals (hours or days – your choice, but you have to be consistent)
Occurrence Rates	For every x stories (or for every x story points)	For every x cards passing a point
Column setup section	Not used	Mandatory
Iteration setup section	Mandatory	Not used

There is no loss of accuracy in whatever process you choose. Some simulation report types aren't supported in one or the other process, but you shouldn't change your development methodology to use any simulation tool; SimML and Focused Objective's tools supports both.

Estimates in SimML

Estimates in SimML follow a specific pattern that supports simulation techniques that employ Monte-carlo techniques. Monte-carlo techniques pick random values between given ranges and run many permutations of a simulation to find likely output patterns. To support this whenever an estimate is called for in SimML, you specify a 90th percentile range estimate in the form of two attributes: `estimateLowBound` and `estimateHighBound`. In Chapter 3 we covered the statistical term 90th percentile range in detail. To recap, it is when an expected actual value has a 90 percent chance of falling within the estimated range; 5% of the actual values are expected to be below the low-bound value, and 5% of actual values are expected to be above the high-bound value.

The examples shown in Listing 5-2 and Listing 5-3 have 90th percentile estimates; in these cases, in the custom backlog definitions and in the Kanban column definitions (repeated here in Listing 5-4 and Listing 5-5 for further discussion). By default, random numbers are chosen using a uniform distribution pattern between the low and high bound values. Listing 5-4 shows there will be 10 stories created in the backlog, and these stories will be assigned a story point size of a value that falls between 1.0 and 3.0 randomly chosen for each of the 10 stories.

Listing 5-4

Example 90th percentile range estimate for Agile/Scrum story size.

```
<backlog type="custom">
        <custom name="Small" count="10"
                estimateLowBound="1" estimateHighBound="3" />
</backlog>
```

Listing 5-5 shows another 90th percentile estimate, this time for column cycle-time. Every story or card that passes through the Design column will be given a cycle-time of a value that lies between 1.0 and 2.0 simulation intervals (whether that be hour or day).

Listing 5-5

Sample 90th percentile range for Lean/Kanban column cycle-time.

```
<columns>
    <column id="1" wipLimit="1"
            estimateLowBound="1" estimateHighBound="2" >
      Design
    </column>
</columns>
```

There are limitations and rules for these estimate values. These rules are enforced by the simulation engine during a validation process prior to executing any simulations, and reported as errors and warnings in the results file. The rules are –

- The value must be numeric.
- The value cannot be omitted or left blank.
- Each value must be > 0.
- The high-bound must be equal-to, or greater-than the low-bound.
- Can only contain a period as the decimal-point character, E.g. 1.5 not 1,5.

Making an Estimate Value Explicit (no range)

For cases where you want to express an actual value to use rather than have a random number chosen at runtime, make the estimateLowBound and estimateHighBound exactly the same value as show in Listing 5-6.

Listing 5-6

To make an estimate an explicit value, make the low-bound exactly the same as the high-bound.

```
<backlog type="custom">
    <custom name="Small" count="10"
            estimateLowBound="3" estimateHighBound="3" />
</backlog>
```

Backlog - Defining the work

The backlog section defines all aspects of the work to be carried out in the project. There are numerous ways of specifying work, and different levels of granularity are available to support getting a quick forecast, and then elaborating on that work in later simulations to obtain a forecast with the certainty you require. For example, you can start by having a single backlog entry with the full count of stories and a single estimate range for the first forecast, and then for later simulations, group stories into groups that are similar size and estimate those groups separately; all the way down to having a single entry and unique estimate for every story.

There are four different types of backlog definition. Each is elaborated on in more detail in this section –

1. Type = simple
   a. Simple Backlog Count (Lean/Kanban only)
2. Type = custom
   b. Percentage Cycle-Time Override (Lean/Kanban only)
   c. Custom Column Cycle-Time Override (Lean/Kanban only)
   d. Custom Story-Point Backlog (Agile/Scrum only)

Lean Simple Backlog Count

The simplest backlog definition is to specify just a number of cards initially populating the backlog. This is a Lean/Kanban only construct. Each card is moved through the Kanban process using the cycle-times specified in the columns section of the SimML file. Listing 5-7 shows the syntax for specifying 30 story cards to initially be placed into the backlog for simulation.

As a starting point for determining that a SimML model is correct in the definition of Kanban columns, WIP limits, this type of backlog is suitable. When looking for more model accuracy, the ability to split the backlog into multiple-groups and have those groups use a specific column cycle-time is important. I suggest using this backlog initially in order to see errors in other parts of the model, and then specify custom backlog entries later in the process.

Listing 5-7

Simple backlog definition for Lean/Kanban models.

```
<setup>
    <backlog type="simple" simpleCount="30" />
    ...
</setup>
```

There is nothing more to explain about this backlog entry. Just remember, character case is important, all first characters are lower-case, and where a new word starts, that letter is upper-case (this type of casing for text is called Camel Casing).

Lean Percentage Cycle-Time Override

If simulating using Lean/Kanban you have the choice of specifying backlog items that use all or part of the cycle-time range defined for each column. To use percentage cycle time overriding, you specify a `percentageLowBound` and a `percentageHighBound` attribute in the custom backlog section as shown in Listing 5-8 .

Listing 5-8

Percentage cycle-time override for backlog entries. Each backlog size uses a segment of the original column range.

```
<backlog type="custom" shuffle="false">
    <custom name="small" count="10"
            percentageLowBound="0"  percentageHighBound="33" />
    <custom name="medium" count="10"
            percentageLowBound="33" percentageHighBound="66" />
    <custom name="large" count="10"
            percentageLowBound="66" percentageHighBound="100" />
</backlog>
```

When simulation takes place, each columns estimation range is used in conjunction with the percentage value to calculate a new low and high bound range that a random number is generated from. The percentage specified relates to the position across the full range of `estimateLowBound` and `estimateHighBound` for a column, and isn't a percentage of the estimate value. The calculation for the low and high bound column estimate value used is –

```
One pct = (column estimateHighBound -
           column estimateLowBound) / 100

low bound value =  column estimateLowBound +
                 (percentageLowBound x one pct)

high bound value =  column estimateLowBound +
                 (percentageHighBound x one pct)
```

For example, if a column has an `estimateLowBound` value of 1 and an `estimate-HighBound` value of 10, a percentage override of 0% would be a value of 1.0, 50% would be a value of 4.5 and 100% would be a value of 10.0. A common mistake is thinking 50% would be 5, but that's not 50% of the original range which is 9 (calculated from `estimateHighBound` – `estimateLowBound`).

Note

You may be asking yourself why the percentage is related to the range rather than just the low and high values. Colum estimates mark the 90th percentile range, and values shouldn't be allowed to occur below the `estimateLowBound` value. If the percentage applied to the low (or high) value, low percentage values would cause values outside of the 90th percentile range, and likely invalid.

To demonstrate one use of percentage overrides, a simple backlog segmentation using segments from the original column ranges can be used. Listing 5-9 shows one implementation where T-Shirt sizing estimates can be used by specifying the low-third of the column range for small stories, the middle-third for medium sized stories, and the top-third for large stories. This type of segmentation of the backlog provides a degree of correlation between the estimates used. Correlation means it makes sense that if a story was quick to develop, it is more probable that it is also quicker to test. Whilst the actual value in the range is still volatile and at the whim of the uniform random number generator, it represents the more real world case and make the simulation output more accurate. Table 5-2 shows the actual value used for each percentage value specified.

Listing 5-9

Percentage override in action segmenting a backlog into small medium and large stories. Column estimates are correlated within these ranges.

```xml
<simulation name="Custom Backlog Test"  >
  <execute>
     <visual />
  </execute>
```

```
<setup>
    <backlog type="custom" shuffle="false">
        <custom name="small" count="10"
            percentageLowBound="0"  percentageHighBound="33" />
        <custom name="medium" count="10"
            percentageLowBound="33" percentageHighBound="66" />
        <custom name="large" count="10"
            percentageLowBound="66" percentageHighBound="100" />
    </backlog>
    <columns>
        <column id="1" estimateLowBound="1" estimateHighBound="10"
                wipLimit="1">Column1</column>
        <column id="2" estimateLowBound="1" estimateHighBound="10"
                wipLimit="1">Column2</column>
        <column id="3" estimateLowBound="1" estimateHighBound="10"
                wipLimit="1">Column3</column>
    </columns>
</setup>
</simulation>
```

Table 5-2

For an original estimate range of 1 to 10, this table shows the actual value used for each percentage override.

Percent value	Value Used
0%	1
33%	3.97
66%	6.94
100%	10

Lean Custom Column Cycle-Time Override

In addition to providing a percentage override for column estimates when simulating Lean/Kanban projects, it is also possible to explicitly give a new cycle-time low and high bound. This can be mixed and matched with the percentage override, which will be used if a column isn't explicitly given a value. The format of custom column cycle-time overriding is to add a column section within the custom backlog section as shown in Listing 5-10. In this example, three columns are overridden (matched by their id value), and given new estimateLowBound and estimateHighBound values.

Listing 5-10

Custom column estimate overrides in a backlog.

```
<backlog type="custom">
    <custom name="risky-first-time-ever-features" count="10">
        <column id="1" estimateLowBound="2" estimateHighBound="5" />
        <column id="2" estimateLowBound="5" estimateHighBound="10" />
        <column id="3" estimateLowBound="3" estimateHighBound="8" />
    </custom>
```

```
</backlog>
```

Not every column needs to be overridden; any omitted columns inherit the cycle-time defined in their column definition. When omitted, a `percentageLowBound` value of 0%, and a `percentageHighBound` value of 100% is used.

This type of backlog definition makes it easier to have a few specific categories of backlog stories that have an emphasis of work in one column or another. This helps make the model more accurate by segmenting specific types of work whilst allowing other columns to inherit the generally accepted 90th percentile range. Listing 5-11 shows one way to specifically use different cycle-times for all columns on risky stories, specifically target a column for more work, and have the remaining stories use the estimate range given for the Kanban columns.

Listing 5-11

Full SimML file showing how to segment a backlog by specific column estimates.

```
<simulation name="Column Override and Inherit Backlog Test" >
  <execute>
     <visual />
  </execute>
  <setup>
   <backlog type="custom">

     <!-- override the first column, the inherit the others -->
     <custom name="design-heavy-stories" count="10">
       <column id="1" estimateLowBound="3" estimateHighBound="5" />
     </custom>

     <!-- override all three -->
     <custom name="first-time-ever-stories"  count="10">
       <column id="1" estimateLowBound="2" estimateHighBound="5"/>
       <column id="2" estimateLowBound="5" estimateHighBound="10"/>
       <column id="3" estimateLowBound="3" estimateHighBound="8" />
     </custom>

     <!-- inherit all columns -->
     <custom name="normal-stories" count="10" />
   </backlog>

   <columns>
       <column id="1" estimateLowBound="1" estimateHighBound="3"
               wipLimit="1">Design</column>
       <column id="2" estimateLowBound="1" estimateHighBound="3"
               wipLimit="2">Develop</column>
       <column id="3" estimateLowBound="1" estimateHighBound="3"
               wipLimit="1">Test</column>
   </columns>
  </setup>
</simulation>
```

Note

Custom column cycle-times allow for exact control over what
cycle-time gets used for every story in every column. It can get
complex if there are too many groups, and it is suggested to only
drop-down to this level of detail with good reason.

Agile Custom Backlog

Agile/Scrum projects use this type of backlog definition. Rest assured though that it's not that Agile/Lean simulation is missing out on any features. Rather, it's just that there is no other place that contains estimations on story size, unlike Lean/Kanban which captures cycle-time in column definitions.

Agile estimates are in points; an artificial unit of measure that aims to be comparative between stories rather than a measure of actual time directly. For each iteration, a certain number of points will be targeted for delivery. When defining the backlog, an estimate-LowBound and estimateHighBound attribute of the custom backlog entry will be the range used when allocating a uniform distributed random number of story points to this story. Listing 5-12 shows the syntax for creating 30 stories, 15 small stories that will be allocated story points between 1.0 and 3.0, 10 stories with points between 3.0 and 10.0 points, and 5 stories with points between 10.0 and 20.0.

Listing 5-12

Agile/Scrum backlog definition in SimML.

```
<backlog type="custom">
    <custom name="small" count="15"
            estimateLowBound="1" estimateHighBound="3" />
    <custom name="medium" count="10"
            estimateLowBound="3" estimateHighBound="10" />
    <custom name="large" count="5"
            estimateLowBound="10" estimateHighBound="20" />
</backlog>
```

Listing 5-12 is an example of how to define a backlog in groups, but every story can be defined individually if stories are estimated in that granularity. Listing 5-13 shows an example where every story is described individually. The estimates can still use low and high bound ranges, or if an exact estimate is wanted, make the estimateLowBound the same value as estimateHighBound.

Listing 5-13

Agile/Scrum backlog with every story estimated.

```
<backlog type="custom">
 <custom name="Story 1"
         estimateLowBound="5" estimateHighBound="8" />
 <custom name="Story 2"
         estimateLowBound="1" estimateHighBound="3" />
```

```
<custom name="Story 3"
        estimateLowBound="5" estimateHighBound="5" />
<custom name="Story 4"
        estimateLowBound="2" estimateHighBound="5" />
   ...
</backlog>
```

Specifying Multiple Deliverables

Software projects are often delivered incrementally rather than the entire backlog in one release. An initial beta release for early-adopters to test and give feedback is made available early whilst development is ongoing, and the final release sometime later. It is necessary to be able to simulate each release separately and combined without having to maintain multiple model files.

To specify a deliverable in the backlog, move the custom backlog sections to within a deliverable section as shown in Listing 5-14. All backlog types support deliverables, the only criteria is that each deliverable section has an opening <deliverable> tag with a name attribute, and is properly closed with an </deliverable> tag before the next deliverable begins. Later in this book we cover how to choose which deliverables are simulated.

Listing 5-14

Any number of deliverables can be defined in the backlog.

```
<backlog type="custom">

    <deliverable name="Beta">
        <custom name="Small" count="6"
                estimateLowBound="1" estimateHighBound="6" />
        <custom name="Medium" count="4"
                estimateLowBound="6" estimateHighBound="12" />
    </deliverable>

    <deliverable name="V1.0">
        <custom name="Small" count="2"
                estimateLowBound="1" estimateHighBound="6" />
        <custom name="Medium" count="2"
                estimateLowBound="6" estimateHighBound="12" />
    </deliverable>

</backlog>
```

Backlog Section Reference

The backlog section is the most complex in SimML because of its support for different development methodologies, and also its ability to be flexible in how granular a backlog contents is described (every story individually to groups of stories, to a simple quantity of stories). Table 5-3 shows the possible section element structures available to define and segment the backlog of work to simulate. Table 5-4, Table 5-5, Table 5-6 and Table 5-7 fully document the attributes allowed within each section.

Table 5-3

Section element structure for the Backlog section.

Element	Description
\<setup>	Mandatory. One per SimML file.
\<backlog ...>	Mandatory. One per SimML file.
\<custom ... />	Custom backlog definition. Mandatory for Agile, optional for Lean.
\<deliverable ...>	Deliverable tags to divide backlog into multiple parts. Optional.
\<custom ... />	Custom backlog embedded inside a deliverable. Optional.
\<custom ... >	Custom backlog with Lean column override. Optional.
\<column ... />	Column Estimate Override. Optional.
\</custom>	Closing tag. Mandatory for every Custom open tag.
\</deliverable>	Closing tag. Mandatory for every Deliverable open tag.
\</backlog>	Closing tag. Mandatory. One per SimML file.
\</setup>	Closing tag. Mandatory. One per SimML file.

Backlog section

Table 5-4

Attribute reference for the Backlog SimML section.

Attribute	Type	Description
nameFormat	string, optional	The format story card names are given. Default is "Story {0}" if omitted. The {0} special character will be replaced with the story cards unique identifier when simulation occurs.
shuffle	true (default), false	Determines if the backlog stories are shuffled into a random order before simulation occurs. Default is true if omitted.
simpleCount	integer	Simple number of story cards to put into the backlog for Lean simulation. Only used when `type="simple"` is defined. Must be > 0 when used.
type	custom (default), simple	The type of backlog definition. Custom is the default value if omitted. When set to simple, the `simpleCount` attribute is used.

Custom section

Table 5-5

Attribute reference for the Custom section of a Backlog SimML section.

Attribute	Type	Description
count	integer, default 1	The number of story cards to add to the backlog with these properties. Default is 1 if omitted. Must be > 0.
estimateLowBound	number	The 5th percentile estimate of story size. This will be the lowest random number selected for stories of this backlog type when simulating. Mandatory if simulating using Agile/Scrum

		simulation type, otherwise ignored. Must not be greater than `estimateHighBound` and must be > 0.
estimateHighBound	number	The 95th percentile estimate of story size. This will be the highest random number selected for stories of this backlog type when simulating. Mandatory if simulating using Agile/Scrum simulation type, otherwise ignored. Must not be less than `estimateLowBound` and must be > 0.
name	string, optional but recommended	The text name of this backlog entry. This is for informational purposes only and is sometimes used in reporting.
percentLowBound	number, default 0	The percentage along a columns estimate range that will be used as the low-bound for random numbers generated for cycle-time for story cards of this backlog type. Value defaults to 0 if omitted, which will mean simulation will use a columns `estimateLowBound` value. Only used when simulating Lean/Kanban projects. Must be > -1 if used. Will be ignored for columns that have explicit column section override in this custom backlog section.
percentHighBound	number, default 100	The percentage along a columns estimate range that will be used as the high-bound for random numbers generated for cycle-time for story cards of this backlog type. Value defaults to 100 if omitted, which will mean simulation will use a columns `estimateHighBound` value. Only used when simulating Lean/Kanban projects. Must be > -1 if used. Will be ignored for columns that have explicit column section override in this custom backlog section.

Column Section

Table 5-6

Attribute reference for a Column section of a Custom SimML section.

Attribute	Type	Description
estimateLowBound	number, mandatory	The 5th percentile estimate of column cycle-time. This will be the lowest random number selected for cycle-time in the Kanban column with the same `id` as this section when simulating. Must not be greater than `estimateHighBound` and must be > 0.
estimateHighBound	number, mandatory	The 95th percentile estimate of column cycle-time. This will be the highest random selected for cycle-time in the Kanban column with the same `id` as this section when simulating. Must not be less than `estimateLowBound` and must be > 0.
id	integer, mandatory	The column id to override cycle-time. There must be a matching column defined with this id value.

Deliverable Section

Table 5-7

Attribute reference for a Deliverable sections of a Backlog SimML section.

Attribute	Type	Description
name	string, optional but recommended	The text name of this deliverable entry. This name is used to choose what backlog entries to include when simulating occurs.

Columns – For Lean/Kanban Methodologies – The journey of work

Lean methodologies pass work through a series of columns or status' during the journey from backlog to complete. The intention is to focus on the throughput of the entire system, and focus on starting and finishing items quickly by reducing or controlling the work in progress (WIP). SimML allows any number of columns to be defined within a columns section in the setup section of the SimML file.

The necessary entries for each column definition are: a name, a unique id, a WIP limit and a low and high bound estimate of cycle time for each work item in a column. When simulating, each card moving through a column will be allocated a work time between the boundaries chosen, and there will never be more than the defined WIP limit number of cards in a column at one time. Listing 5-15 shows a typical column definition section.

Listing 5-15

Lean/Kanban Column definitions.

```
<setup>
  <columns>
    <column id="1" estimateLowBound="1" estimateHighBound="3"
            wipLimit="2">Graphics-Design</column>
    <column id="2" estimateLowBound="1" estimateHighBound="3"
            wipLimit="2">UI-Code</column>
    <column id="3" estimateLowBound="1" estimateHighBound="3"
            wipLimit="3">Server-Side Code</column>
    <column id="4" estimateLowBound="1" estimateHighBound="3"
            wipLimit="2">QA</column>
  </columns>
</setup>
```

Table 5-8 documents the allowed attributes for each of the `column` elements.

Table 5-8
Reference for the Column SimML section, which must be contained within a Columns section.

Attribute	Type	Description
estimateLowBound	number, mandatory	The 5th percentile estimate of cycle-time. Random numbers will not be produced below this value. Must be > 0 and less than or equal `estimateHighBound`.
estimateHighBound	number, mandatory	The 95th percentile estimate of cycle-time. Random numbers will not be produced above this value. Must be > 0 and greater than or equal `estimateLowBound`.
id	integer, mandatory	A unique column identifier as an integer number. Columns will be ordered from lowest id value to the highest.
buffer	false (default), true	If a column is a buffer it is skipped if there is a vacant position in the next column. If there is no vacant position on the next column, cards are queued in this position. WIP limit still applies. No estimates are needed, it will always be 0.
wipLimit	integer, mandatory	The limit of stories/cards allowed in this column at one time. Must be > 0.
Value within the column element	text	The name of the column. Avoid using less-than (<) and greater-than (>) signs within the name of the column.

Column order for simulation is based upon the ascending order of the id values, not the physical order in the file. Although the id values can be any integer number (no decimal places), start from 1 and then 2, 3, and 4 and so on to make referencing these numbers easier in other parts of the model. These column id values are used when referencing these columns in other sections of the model (allowing the column names to change without breaking the model referencing).

Buffer and Queuing Columns

Some columns in Kanban aren't used for work; they are used to buffer and queue work in other columns. Cards moved into these columns are immediately eligible to move to the next column if there is an open position. Buffer columns are used to improve flow through the Kanban system by allowing work to be buffered and queued for constrained or non-immediately available resources.

To specify a column as a buffer, add a `buffer="true"` attribute to that column definition. Listing 5-16 demonstrates how to make two columns queue and buffer the following column in a Kanban board. The first column "Requirements Ready" will always be populated with three items from the backlog or the defects backlog. The "Ready to Test" column will only hold a story card if there is no open positions in the "Test" column.

Listing 5-16

Buffer columns are defined with the buffer="true" attribute.

```
<simulation name="Buffer column example" >
  <execute>
    <visual />
  </execute>
  <setup>
    <backlog type="simple" simpleCount="50" />
    <columns>
        <column id="1" buffer="true" wipLimit="3">
            Requirements Ready</column>
        <column id="2" estimateLowBound="1" estimateHighBound="3"
                wipLimit="2">
            Develop</column>
        <column id="3" buffer="true" wipLimit="3">
            Ready to Test</column>
        <column id="4" estimateLowBound="1" estimateHighBound="5"
                wipLimit="1">
            Test</column>
    </columns>
  </setup>
</simulation>
```

Figure 5-3
Buffer columns have a different icon on the empty board (white background with small tick mark)

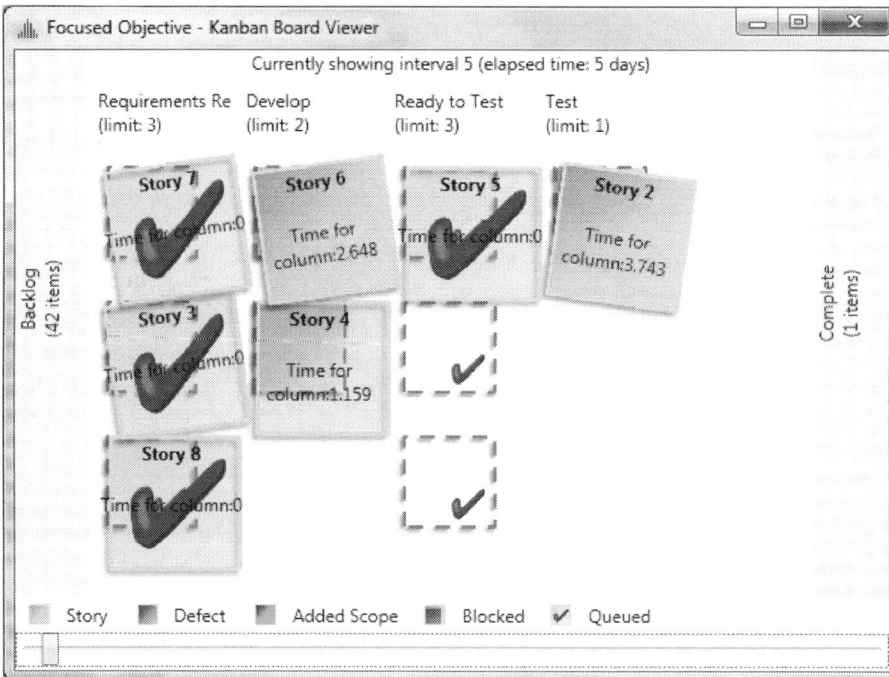

Buffer column positions are shown on the Kanban visualizer as dashed-squares with a white background with a small red tick-mark in the bottom right hand corner. Traditional empty positions have a gray background and no tick-mark. Figure 5-3 shows the resulting Kanban board with buffer columns as defined in Listing 5-16.

When a card is moved into a buffered position, the following rules apply –

- If there is an open position in the next column, move the card immediately.

- If no open position exists in the next column, mark the card as complete.

- If there are any open positions in the first column, and if it is a buffered column, fill as many positions as possible from defects and then backlog.

Iteration – For Agile/Iterative Methodologies – How much, how often

Agile methodologies like Scrum deliver work progressively in iterations. These iterations are time-boxed, often to two weeks, but other units of time are sometimes used in practice to support a local release cadence requirement.

Listing 5-17 shows an example iteration section in SimML. The attributes specify how many days you are using for iterations, and the 90th percentile range for the number of story points to allocate each simulated iteration.

Listing 5-17

Iteration definition in SimML.

```
<setup>
  <iteration workDaysPerIteration="10"
          storyPointsPerIterationLowBound="10"
          storyPointsPerIterationHighBound="15"  />
  ...
</setup>
```

At the beginning of each simulated iteration, a uniformly distributed random number is chosen from between the values specified in the `storyPointsPerIterationLowBound` and `storyPointsPerIterationHighBound` attributes. Stories are then picked from the backlog until this random number of points to be allocated in this iteration is exceeded. It is possible to restrict the allocation of work to always be under the target points by adding the optional attribute: `allowedToOverAllocate="false"`.

> **Note**
>
> To make the number of points per iteration explicit, make the `storyPointsPerIterationLowBound` and `storyPoints-PerIterationLowBound` attributes the same value.

Table 5-9 documents the allowed attributes for the `iteration` element.

Table 5-9

Reference for the Iteration SimML section, which must be contained within a setup section.

Attribute	Type/Values	Description
allowedToOverAllocate	true (default), false	Determines if the simulation engine can exceed the number of story points per iteration by the excess points in one story, or whether it must be below the target value. Defaults to true if omitted.
storyPointsPerIteration HighBound	number, mandatory	The 95th percentile estimate of target points to allocate for each simulated iteration. Random numbers will not be produced above this value. Must be > 0 and greater than `storyPointsPerIterationLowBound`.
storyPointsPerIteration LowBound	number, mandatory	The 5th percentile estimate of target points to allocate for each simulated iteration. Random numbers will not be produced below this value. Must be > 0 and less than `storyPointsPerIterationHighBound`.
workDaysPerIteration	integer (default of 10)	The number of calendar workdays for each simulated iteration. Defaults to 10 if omitted. Must be > 0.

Summary

This chapter introduced the Simulation Modeling Language (SimML) modeling elements that are required to simulate and forecast. The next chapters look at expanding from these basic SimML file elements to include other events that happen during software development in order to make our models more complete and accurately reflect the real-world.

Chapter 6
Modeling Development Events

What makes SimML such a powerful language is that it supports an event driven model for real-world events that occur during software development. The ability to model and simulate the compounding impact of these events is what makes these models much more accurate than simple a spreadsheet. This chapter explains how to define these events in a SimML model.

Development Event Types

During the software development process, many events occur that add additional work to a project and this is the major reason that traditional spreadsheet estimation and forecasting has proven to be erroneous and misleading. These events have to be modeled in order to simulate their compounding effect if an accurate forecast is to be generated. Any type of software development event can be modeled using three simple structures in SimML –

1. *Added Scope*: Work that gets added to the project after it begins. Some examples are refactoring work that developers need to carry out and new ideas and changes added by business stake holders.
2. *Blocking Events*: Events that cause a story card to sit idle for a period of time. Some examples are waiting for answers to questions and testing environments that aren't immediately available.
3. *Defects*: Work that gets created to rework prior completed work. Some examples are defects in functionality found by QA and defects that happen in production and need immediate attention.

Although each event type is different, they share a common trait of how occurrence rate is specified.

Event Occurrence Rates

SimML supports defining events that occur at estimated rates. For example, defects might be added to the backlog at a certain rate to simulate the real world of bug finding and fixing. Whenever an occurrence rate is defined in SimML it takes the form of a range of either the number of story cards passing a point, or the number of story points being completed. Three attributes allow these occurrence rate estimates to be defined, they are: `occurrenceType`, `occurrenceLowBound` and `occurrenceHighBound`.

The occurrence low bound and high bound operate the same way as estimates, they represent the 90th percentile range. The code in Listing 6-1 would trigger the event between the 5th story and the 10th story or card completed; the exact story or card being chosen at random between those bounds.

Listing 6-1

An example event definition using occurrence rate by story card count.

```
<addedScopes>
    <addedScope occurrenceType="count"
        occurrenceLowBound="5"
        occurrenceHighBound="10" … >Scope Creep {0}</addedScope>
</addedScopes>
```

The occurrence rate low and high bounds do have some rules. These rules are enforced by the simulation engine during a validation process prior to executing any simulations, and reported as errors and warnings in the results file. The rules are –

- The value must be numeric.
- The value cannot be omitted or left blank.
- Each value must be > 0.
- The high-bound must be equal-to, or greater-than the low-bound.
- Can only contain a decimal-point as a period, E.g. 1.5 not 1,5.

The occurrence bounds are one part of the rate definition. What unit of measure these bounds are is controlled by the `occurrenceType` value. There are three occurrence types supported –

1. *Count*: The number of story cards that are completed for every event triggered (or for Kanban, the number of story cards that pass through a column).
2. *Percentage*: The percentage of story cards that are completed for every event triggered (or for Kanban, the number of story cards that pass through a column).
3. *Size* (Agile/Scrum only): The number of story points completed for every event triggered.

Each individual event can use a different occurrence type, there is no need to pick one and use it for every event in a SimML file. Each occurrence type will now be covered in detail.

Count Occurrence Rate– 1 in x Story Cards

When the `occurrenceType` attribute value is `count`, the simulation engine counts the number of story cards passing a point and triggers the event in question after a certain number is reached. It can be the number of story cards being started, or completed depending on the event type itself. This is the default occurrence rate type if no other type is specified. Listing 6-1 demonstrates how an occurrence rate based on story card count is defined.

Events using this type of occurrence rate trigger once ever number of story cards defined. For example, a value of 1 would mean every story card triggers an event; a value of 2 would be every 2nd, and 3 every 3rd story card. The actual number to trigger the event will be a uniform random number between the low bound and the high bound, unless the low-bound and high-bound values are the same when that value is used explicitly.

One important point when looking at occurrence rates specified using the count type is that the smaller the number, the more frequent an event. This might feel counter-intuitive specifying the low-bound which actually means "more-often", but the simulation engine is picking a random-number between the bounds chosen, and it needs to know that the low-bound is less than the high-bound value – you are specifying the range which a random number will be chosen between, not the exact value.

Percentage Occurrence Rate – x% of story cards

It might be more convenient to specify event occurrence rate using percentage. This is similar to specifying the occurrence rate as a count, but in percentage form. 100% would mean every story card triggers an event, 50% would mean every 2nd story card, and 33% every 3rd story card. Listing 6-2 demonstrates how to define an occurrence rate using percentage values. In this case an event is triggered at a random percentage between 25% and 50% of story cards passing. This equates to between 1 in 4 and 1 in 2 cards.

Unlike the count type, the low-bound percentage value represents a less-frequent event occurrence (50% is less often than 100% of the time). The simulation engine behind the scenes converts these percentages into a 1 in x story count value, and this type is available for convenience only.

This occurrence type is often convenient when initially prototyping a model; it is often easier for experts to think in 50% of story cards, or 33% of story cards. Once real data is flowing through a project, measuring the occurrence rate should give more accurate ratios of story cards passing a point versus how many certain events occur.

Listing 6-2

An example event definition using occurrence rate by story card percentage.

```
<addedScopes>
    <addedScope occurrenceType="percentage"
                occurrenceLowBound="25"
                occurrenceHighBound="50" … >Scope Creep {0}
    </addedScope>
</addedScopes>
```

Size Occurrence Rate – x story points

Agile/Scrum projects have the option of specifying events to occur once for a given number of story points. Rather than story cards passing a point being counted, the story points are summed, and when they reach the occurrence value, the event is triggered. Listing 6-3 shows an example event definition where the event will trigger after a random-value between 10 and 20 story points are started.

This type of occurrence rate has the benefit of reflecting the correlation that larger pieces of work stand a higher chance of triggering more events. For example, bigger stories will more likely have more defects reported against them during testing.

When specifying occurrence rate by size, the low-bound and high-bound occurrence values are the boundaries for a uniform random number to be selected. The simulation engine watches for every card being started or completed (depending on the event) and keeps a running total of the story points. When the number of points exceeds the random value selected, the event is triggered. Excess story points are carried over to the sum for the next event, ensuring that over the full simulation, the correct number of events triggered will be mathematically accurate.

Listing 6-3

An example event definition using occurrence rate by story card size.

```
<addedScopes>
    <addedScope occurrenceType="size"
        occurrenceLowBound="10"
        occurrenceHighBound="20" … >Scope Creep {0}</addedScope>
</addedScopes>
```

Making an Occurrence Rate an Explicit Value

In a similar fashion to the 90th percentile range estimates used for defining columns cycle-times and backlog sizes, to force an explicit value to be used, make the occurrenceLowBound equal the value of the occurrenceHighBound. When the simulation engine sees this configuration, it uses that number rather than calling the random number generator for a value. Listing 6-4 shows how to explicitly trigger an event every 5th card being completed.

Listing 6-4

An example event definition using occurrence rate by story card count showing how to force an explicit value rather than a random value between low and high bounds.

```
<addedScopes>
    <addedScope occurrenceType="count"
            occurrenceLowBound="5"
            occurrenceHighBound="5" … >Scope Creep {0}
    </addedScope>
</addedScopes>
```

Added Scope

Added scope events create more work in the project backlog at given occurrence rates. These events can be used to simulate how project scope increases due to changing requirements, more defined requirements or un-anticipated developer work (refactoring being a common case).

Lean/Kanban Added Scope Events

When added scope events trigger, new story cards are added to the end of the backlog. These cards will flow through the Lean/Kanban columns after all other work is completed, using the cycle-times defined for each column. For Lean/Kanban simulation, the count of the story cards occurs when they are completed (move from the last column into the completed list).

Listing 6-5 shows two added scope events being created in the SimML languauge; one to represent increasing scope due to new features being added, and one developer refactoring work as the project progresses. Both added scope events will occur at the same rate, between 1 in 4 and 1 in 10 story cards being completed (defined here in this way to demonstrate how to use both types of occurrence rate definition).

Listing 6-5

Added scope event definitions for Lean/Kanban simulation. This example creates two added scope events.

```
<addedScopes>
    <addedScope occurrenceLowBound="4"
            occurrenceHighBound="10">Scope Creep {0}
    </addedScope>

    <addedScope occurrenceType="percentage"
            occurenceLowBound="10"
            occurenceHighBound="25">Refactoring {0}</addedScope>
</addedScopes>
```

The special placeholder {0} in an added scope event's name is replaced at simulation time with a unique identifier for the card just created. It is optional, but useful when viewing these events in the Kanban Board Viewer to avoid all added scope cards having the same name. Figure 6-1 shows the added scope cards on the Kanban board. Notice there different color (green rather than yellow – apologies if you are reading a black and white copy of this book) and their names after the placeholder is replaced with a unique value.

Figure 6-1

Kanban Board Viewer showing added scope story cards being completed. Notice the {0} special character has been replaced with a unique identifier number.

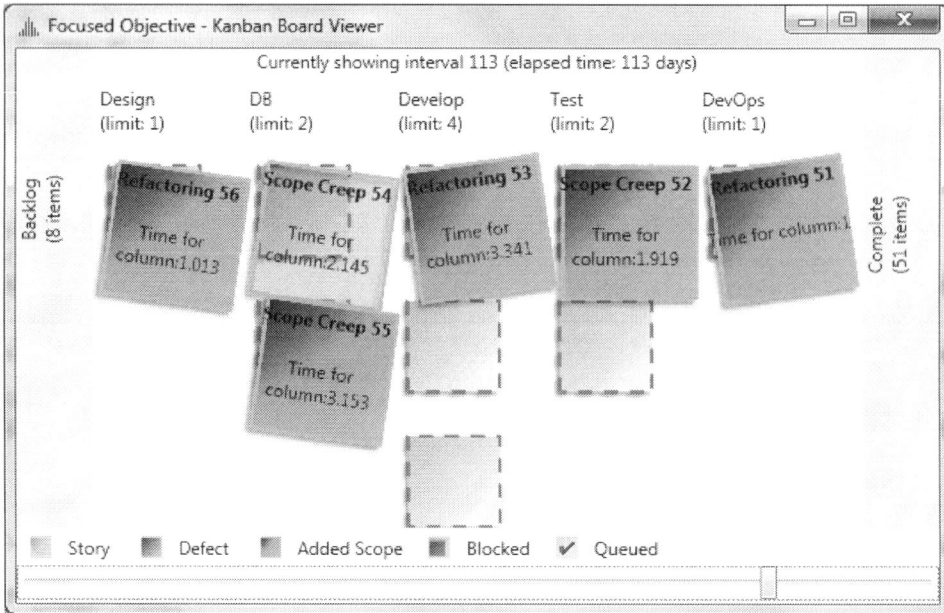

Agile/Scrum Added Scope Events

Added scope events for Agile/Scrum projects are identical to those created for Lean/Kanban with the addition of an estimate for story size. The estimates provide the simulation engine with the story size to populate the new backlog items on creation, and are specified in the `estimateLowBound` and `estimateHighBound` attributes of the added scope element section.

All of the occurrence types are available, count, percentage and size. Examples of each occurrence type are shown in Listing 6-6. The low and high-bound estimate attributes are the tell-tale sign this is an Agile/Scrum project file.

Listing 6-6

Added scope event definitions for Agile/Scrum simulation. This example creates three added scope events.

```
<addedScopes>
  <addedScope   count="2" occurrenceType="count"
    occurrenceLowBound="4" occurrenceHighBound="10"
    estimateLowBound="3" estimateHighBound="5">
  Scope Creep {0}</addedScope>

  <addedScope   occurrenceType="percentage"
    occurrenceLowBound="10" occurrenceHighBound="25"
    estimateLowBound="3" estimateHighBound="5">
  Scope Creep {0}</addedScope>
```

```
<addedScope occurrenceType="size"
    occurrenceLowBound="2.5" occurrenceHighBound="5.5"
    estimateLowBound="2" estimateHighBound="5">
  Refactoring {0}</addedScope>
</addedScopes>
```

Added scope items are put at the end of the backlog, and will be added to iterations after all of the original work items and defects have been completed. The {0} special character in the name value for each added scope event is replaced by a unique identifier during simulation. Figure 6-2 shows the added scope story cards in the Scrum Board Viewer after simulation.

Figure 6-2

Scrum Board Viewer showing added scope story cards being completed. Notice the {0} special character has been replaced with a unique identifier number.

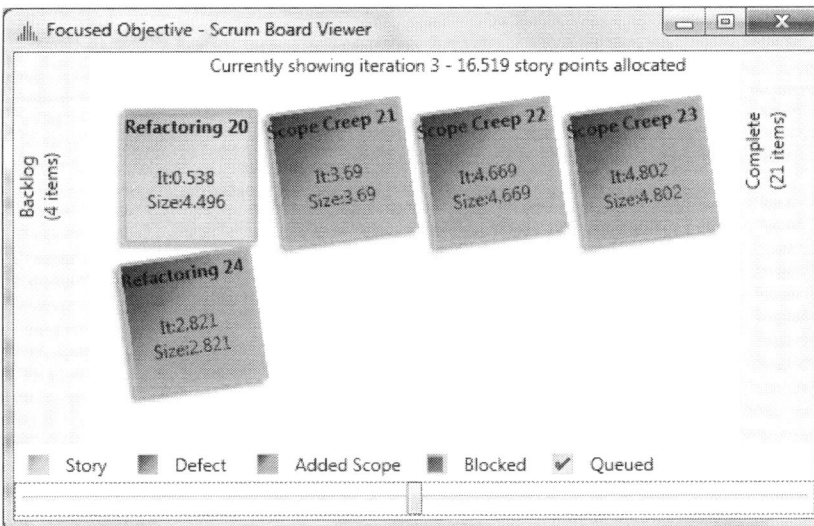

Added Scope Section Reference

There can be one or more `addedScope` section elements within the `addedScopes` section that is contained within the `setup` section of a SimML file as described in Table 6-1.

Table 6-1

Section element structure for the Added Scopes section.

Element	Description
<setup>	Mandatory. One per SimML file.
<addedScopes>	Optional. One per SimML file.
<addedScope ... >	One or more added scope event definitions.
name	The name of the added scope event. Use {0} for unique event id.
</addedScope>	Closing tag. Mandatory one for every added scope event.
</addedScopes>	Closing tag. Mandatory. One per SimML file.

</setup>	Closing tag. Mandatory. One per SimML file.

Table 6-2 shows the fully documented attributes that are allowed for each added scope event defined.

Table 6-2

The attributes allowed for the Added Scope section of the Setup section of a SimML file.

Attribute	Type	Description
count	integer, default 1	The number of story cards to add to the backlog with these properties. Default is 1 if omitted. Must be > 0.
estimateLowBound	number, mandatory for Agile/Scrum otherwise ignored	The 5th percentile estimate of story size for the stories added by this event. This will be the lowest random number selected for story size of this added scope when simulating. Mandatory if simulating using Agile/Scrum simulation type, otherwise ignored. Must be less than or equal estimateHighBound and must be > 0.
estimateHighBound	number, mandatory for Agile/Scrum otherwise ignored	The 95th percentile estimate of story size for the stories added by this event. This will be the highest random number selected for story size of this added scope when simulating. Mandatory if simulating using Agile/Scrum simulation type, otherwise ignored. Must be more than or equal estimateLowBound and must be > 0.
occurrenceLowBound	number, mandatory	The low-bound of occurrence rate estimate. The unit of measure of this number will vary depending on what occurrenceType is specified. Must be less than or equal occurrenceHighBound and must be > 0.
occurrenceHighBound	number, mandatory	The high-bound of occurrence rate estimate. The unit of measure of this number will vary depending on what occurrenceType is specified. Must be greater than or equal occurrenceLowBound and must be > 0.
occurrenceType	count (default), percentage or size	The unit of measure that the occurrence rate is specified. The default value is count if omitted.
section element value	string	The text name for this backlog entry. The special string {0} will be replaced at simulation time by an unique identifier.

Blocking Events

Blocking events are used to delay the progress of work being completed on a story card for a certain amount of time. Some examples of blocking events are when work is impeded awaiting the answer to a question or when a test environment is un-available. During simulation, if a story card is chosen to be blocked; extra time is added to the completion time for that story in the iteration or in the cycle-time of the column.

Lean/Kanban Blocking Events

Blocking events for Lean/Kanban projects are triggered in a chosen column. The column is defined by matching the `columnId` attribute of the blocking event with an `id` in a `column` defined in the `columns` section (see Chapter 5).

The `lowBoundEstimate` and `highBoundEstimate` attribute values specify the range for a random number to be chosen from. The value of this random number is the amount of additional cycle-time added to triggered story cards when they move through the column defined with the matching `columnId` identifier.

The occurrence rate types of `count` (the type used if `occurrenceType` is omitted) and `percentage` are supported for Lean/Kanban projects, and cards are counted when they move into the chosen column.

Listing 6-7 demonstrates how to define two blocking events. These events target different columns, the first the development column where randomly chosen story cards occurring between 1 in 4 and 1 in 10 cards passing into this column will be blocked for an additional cycle-time of a random number between 1 and 3 simulation units (hours or days). The second blocking event occurs at the same rate of between 1 in 4 and 1 in 10 story cards, but it targets the QA column, and will block for between 1 and 2 hours or days (depending on what units are specified in the SimML file).

Listing 6-7

Blocking event definitions for Lean/Kanban simulation. This example creates two blocking events showing the difference occurrence rates available.

```
<blockingEvents>
    <blockingEvent columnId="3"
        occurrenceLowBound="4" occurrenceHighBound="10"
        estimateLowBound="1" estimateHighBound="3">
     Block dev (missing requirement)
    </blockingEvent>

    <blockingEvent columnId="4" occurrenceType="percentage"
        occurrenceLowBound="10" occurrenceHighBound="25"
        estimateLowBound="1" estimateHighBound="2">
     Block testing (environment down)
    </blockingEvent>
</blockingEvents>

<columns>
  <column id="1" …>Design</column>
  <column id="2" …>DB</column>
  <column id="3" …>Develop</column>
  <column id="4" …>Test</column>
  <column id="5" …>DevOps</column>
</columns>
```

Figure 6-3 show how blocking events are shown in the Kanban Board Viewer for a simulation run.

Figure 6-3

Kanban Board Viewer showing blocking events occurring on a story cards.

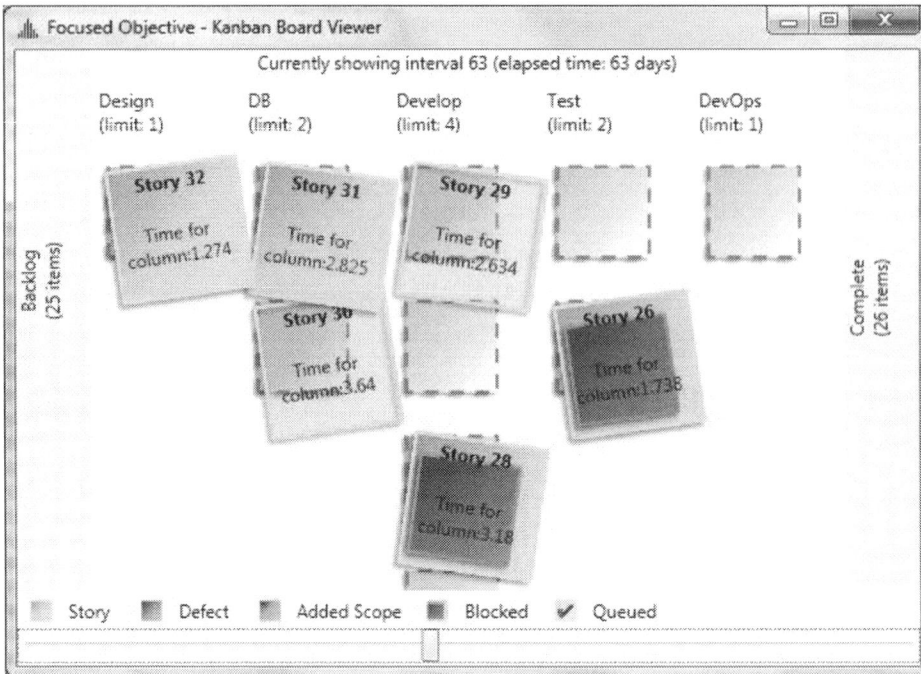

Agile/Scrum Blocking Events

When simulating blocking events for Agile/Scrum projects, the estimate low-bound and high-bound value is the amount of extra story points to add to a story if triggered by an event. There is no need to specify a `columnId` either, and if this is specified it is ignored.

Listing 6-8 demonstrates how to define three blocking events using the difference `occurrenceType` attribute values.

Listing 6-8

Blocking event definitions for Agile/Scrum simulation. This example creates three blocking events showing the difference occurrence rates available.

```
<blockingEvents>
    <blockingEvent occurrenceType="count"
        occurrenceLowBound="4" occurrenceHighBound="10"
        estimateLowBound="1" estimateHighBound="3">Block - Question
    </blockingEvent>

    <blockingEvent occurrenceType="percentage"
        occurrenceLowBound="10" occurrenceHighBound="25"
        estimateLowBound="1" estimateHighBound="2">Block - Vacation
    </blockingEvent>

    <blockingEvent occurrenceType="size"
```

```
      occurrenceLowBound="2.5" occurrenceHighBound="5.5"
      estimateLowBound="1" estimateHighBound="2">
    Block - No test envir.
  </blockingEvent>
</blockingEvents>
```

Figure 6-4 shows how Blocking Events are displayed in the Scrum Board Viewer after simulation.

Figure 6-4
Scrum Board Viewer showing blocking events occurring on a story cards.

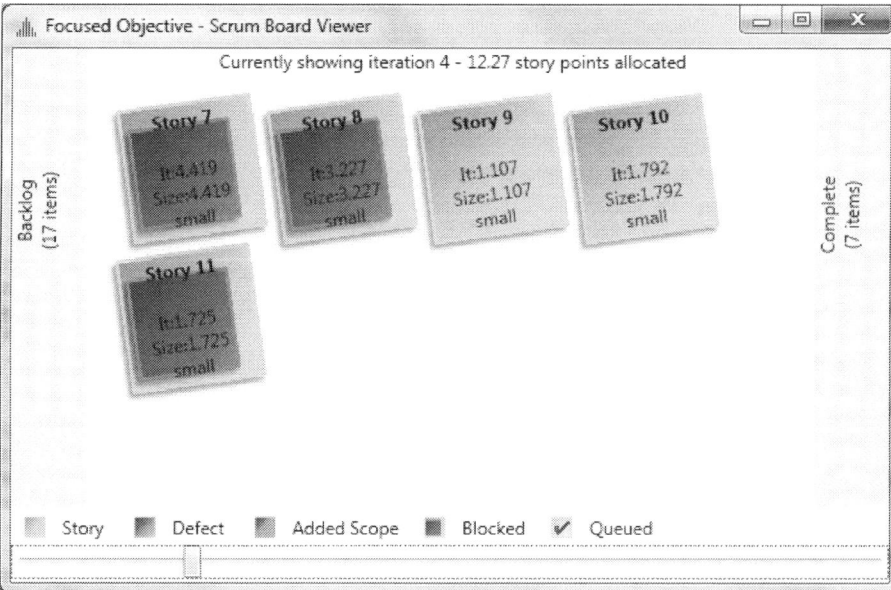

Blocking Event Section Reference

There can be one or more `blockingEvent` section elements within the `blockingEvents` section that is contained within the `setup` section of a SimML file as described in Table 6-3.

Table 6-3
Section element structure for the Blocking Events section.

Element	Description
<setup>	Mandatory. One per SimML file.
<blockingEvents>	Optional. One per SimML file.
<blockingEvent … >	One or more added blocking event definitions.
name	The name of the blocking event.
</blockingEvent>	Closing tag. Mandatory one for every blocking event.
</blockingEvents>	Closing tag. Mandatory. One per SimML file.
</setup>	Closing tag. Mandatory. One per SimML file.

Table 6-4 shows the fully documented attributes that are allowed for each blocking event.

Table 6-4

The attributes allowed for the Blocking Event section of the Setup section of a SimML file.

Attribute	Type	Description
columnId	integer, mandatory for Lean/Kanban	The column the blocking event will occur in. A matching column `id` must be found in the setup columns section. Ignored for Agile/Lean projects.
estimateLowBound	number, mandatory	The 5th percentile estimate of blocked time or size. This will be the lowest random number selected for block cycle-time or story points added when simulating. Must be less than or equal `estimateHighBound` and must be > 0.
estimateHighBound	number, mandatory	The 95th percentile estimate of blocked time or size. This will be the highest random number selected for block cycle-time or story points added when simulating. Must be greater than or equal `estimateLowBound` and must be > 0.
occurrenceLowBound	number, mandatory	The low-bound of occurrence estimate. This number will vary depending on what `occurrenceType` is specified. Must be less than or equal `occurrence-HighBound` and must be > 0.
occurrenceHighBound	number, mandatory	The high-bound of occurrence estimate. This number will vary depending on what `occurrenceType` is specified. Must be greater than or equal `occurrenceLowBound` and must be > 0.
occurrenceType	count (default), percentage or size	The unit of measure that the occurrence rate is specified. The default value is count if omitted.
section element value	string	The text name for this blocking event entry. Not currently used anywhere during simulation, but useful in the SimML file for identification of what each blocking event is for.

Defects

Defect events add story cards to the backlog or a column based on the rate of other work story cards, and these defect stories get priority in the backlog (defects get worked on as soon as possible). Defects represent work being re-opened either in the backlog or in a Kanban column of your choice.

Lean/Kanban Defect Events

Defects are the most feature rich of the events that can be defined in SimML. Defects can be triggered in any column, and can create new work beginning in any column. For example, a defect can be found in testing that creates the next story card to be prioritized as the next piece of work take in the development column.

Lean/Kanban defects are triggered after the specified number of story cards are started in the column with the same identifier as specified in the `columnId` attribute value. If -1 is the value specified for the `columnId` attribute value, the number of story cards completed is counted.

When triggered, the number of stories indicated in the `count` attribute value is created in the column with the identifier matching the value in the `startInColumnId` attribute. If -1 is specified for the `startsInColumnId` attribute value, the defect stories are created in the backlog. In all cases, these defects get priority over other work during simulation (they go first).

Defect stories use the cycle-time specified for each column unless overridden in the defect section using column override sections; one for every column (or at least all columns from and after that specified in the `startsInColumId` attribute).

Listing 6-9 demonstrates how to create two defect events. The first shows how to utilize the default story card count occurrence rate, and shows 2 defects get created after 1 in 2 to 1 in 5 cards move into the Testing column. These defects are the next work allocated in the DB column. The second defect triggers after 10% to 20% of story cards move into the DevOps column. A single defect is the next piece of work to move into the Develop column, and the cycle-times specified in this defects column sections are used instead of each columns specified cycle-time estimates.

Listing 6-9

Defect event definitions for Lean/Kanban simulation. This example creates two defect events showing the difference occurrence rates available.

```
<defects>
  <defect columnId="4" startsInColumnId="2" count="2"
          occurrenceLowBound="2" occurrenceHighBound="5">
    Bug found in Testing ({0})
  </defect>

  <defect columnId="5" startsInColumnId="3"
          occurrenceType="percentage"
          occurrenceLowBound="10" occurrenceHighBound="20">
    Bug found in Dev Ops ({0})
    <column id="3" estimateLowBound="1" estimateHighBound="2" />
    <column id="4" estimateLowBound="1" estimateHighBound="1.5" />
    <column id="5" estimateLowBound="1" estimateHighBound="1" />
  </defect>
</defects>
<columns>
  <column id="1" …>Design</column>
  <column id="2" …>DB</column>
  <column id="3" …>Develop</column>
  <column id="4" …>Test</column>
  <column id="5" …>DevOps</column>
</columns>
```

The name for each defect story is the value of the defect section element itself and it can contain the special string {0} which is replaced at simulation time with a unique identifier for this story card defect. The special string is optional, but it is useful for tracking the defects visually on the simulation board. Figure 6-5 shows how defect events are shown in the Kanban Board Viewer for a simulation run, including how the special string is replaced.

Figure 6-5
Kanban Board Viewer showing defect events occurring on a story cards.

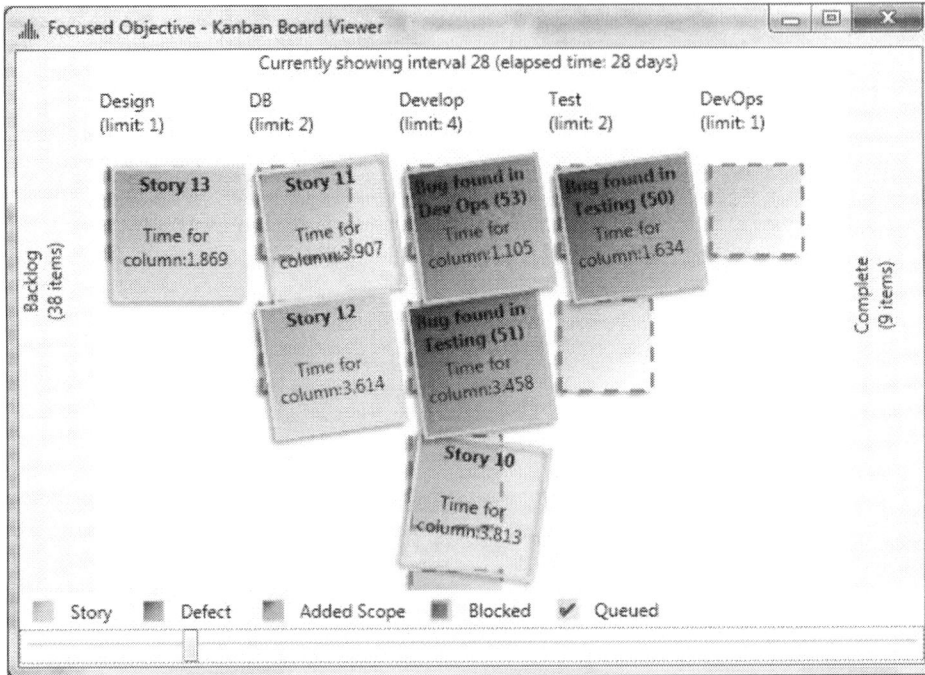

Agile/Scrum Defect Events

Defect events in Agile/Scrum are straightforward and act similar to addedScope events except that they are put at the front of the queue of the backlog rather than at the end. Defects that get triggered take priority over other backlog work in the next iteration.

All of the occurrence types are valid for defect event definition. If the occurrence-Type attribute value is omitted, the occurrence type of count is used.

A number of defects can be created when one event triggers by specifying a value in the count attribute. If this is omitted, a single defect is added. Defects that are created are assigned a story point value that falls within the range specified in the estimateLowBound and estimateHighBound attribute values.

Listing 6-10 demonstrates how to create three defect events. Each example uses one of the three occurrence types available. The special string of {0} in the name definition (the value of the defect element) is replaced at simulation time with a unique identifier for the defect being created. It is optional but useful when following work visually in the Scrum Board Viewer.

Listing 6-10

Defect event definitions for Agile/Scrum simulation. This example creates three defect events.

```
<defects>
  <defect count="2" occurrenceLowBound="4" occurrenceHighBound="10"
      estimateLowBound="1" estimateHighBound="3">
  Bug found in Testing ({0})
  </defect>

  <defect occurrenceType="percentage"
      occurrenceLowBound="10" occurrenceHighBound="25"
      estimateLowBound="1" estimateHighBound="1" >
  Bug in CSS Code ({0})
  </defect>

  <defect  occurrenceType="size"
     occurrenceLowBound="2.5" occurrenceHighBound="5.5"
     estimateLowBound="1" estimateHighBound="2" >
  Bug in DevOps ({0})
  </defect>
</defects>
```

Figure 6-6 shows the added scope story cards in the Scrum Board Viewer after simulation.

Figure 6-6
Scrum Board Viewer showing defect story cards being completed. Notice the {0} special character has been replaced with a unique identifier number.

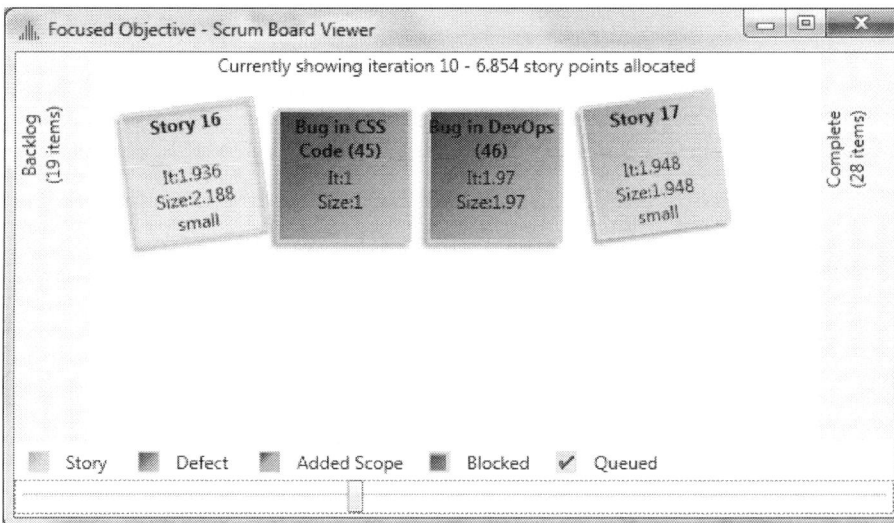

Defect Event Section Reference

There can be one or more `defect` section elements within the `defects` section that is contained within the `setup` section of a simML file as described in Table 6-5.

Table 6-5
Section element structure for the Defects section.

Element	Description
<setup>	Mandatory. One per SimML file.
<defects>	Optional. One per SimML file.
<defect ... >	One or more defect event definitions.
name	The name of the defect event. Use {0} for unique event id.
<column ... />	Optional. One or more column cycle-time override (Kanban only).
</defect>	Closing tag. Mandatory one for every defect event.
</defects>	Closing tag. Mandatory. One per SimML file.
</setup>	Closing tag. Mandatory. One per SimML file.

Table 6-6 shows the fully documented attributes that are allowed for each defect event. Table 6-7 shows the attributes that are allowed for each column cycle-time override if used and if simulating a Lean/Kanban project.

Table 6-6
The attributes allowed for the Defect section of the Setup section of a SimML file.

Attribute	Type	Description
count	integer, default 1	The number of defect story cards to create. Default is 1 if omitted. Must be > 0.
estimateLowBound	number, mandatory for Agile/Scrum otherwise ignored	The 5th percentile estimate of story size for the stories added by this event. This will be the lowest random number selected for story size of these defects when simulating. Mandatory if simulating using Agile/Scrum simulation type, otherwise ignored. Must not be greater than `estimateHighBound` and must be > 0.
estimateHighBound	number, mandatory for Agile/Scrum otherwise ignored	The 95th percentile estimate of story size for the stories added by this event. This will be the highest random number selected for story size of these defects when simulating. Mandatory if simulating using Agile/Scrum simulation type, otherwise ignored. Must not be less than `estimateLowBound` and must be > 0.
occurrenceLowBound	number, mandatory	The low-bound of occurrence rate estimate. The unit of measure of this number will vary depending on what `occurrenceType` is specified. Must be less than `occurrenceHighBound` and must be > 0.
occurrenceHighBound	number, mandatory	The high-bound of occurrence rate estimate. The unit of measure of this number will vary depending on what `occurrenceType` is specified. Must be greater than `occurrenceLowBound` and must be > 0.
occurrenceType	count (default),	The unit of measure that the occurrence rate is specified.

	percentage or size	The default value is count if omitted.
section element value	string	The text name for these defects. The special string {0} will be replaced at simulation time by a unique identifier.

Table 6-7

The attributes allowed for the Column cycle-time override section of a Defect section.

Attribute	Type	Description
estimateLowBound	number, mandatory	The 5th percentile estimate of cycle-time for defects in the column with the same id value. Random numbers will not be produced below this value. Must be > 0 and not more than `estimateHighBound`.
estimateHighBound	number, mandatory	The 95th percentile estimate of cycle-time for defects in the column with the same id value. Random numbers will not be produced above this value. Must be > 0 and not less than `estimateLowBound`.
id	integer, mandatory	The column identifier to override cycle-time. This id value must match a defined column id value.

Summary

This chapter has described how to create one or more of the optional development events in SimML models. These events allow the real-world impact of defects, project scope-creep and impediments to progress to be modeled and simulated giving more accurate forecasts.

Chapter 5 and 6 have covered how to model a software project using the SimML language. The upcoming chapters cover how to execute simulations using these models in order to get forecasts and information to make better decisions about a project schedule, cost and staffing requirements.

Chapter 7
Executing Simulations

In Chapter 5 we covered the basic structure of a SimML file – two main sections: Setup and Execute. We have covered the Setup section in detail over the past two chapters and this chapter covers the Execute section. The execute section of the SimML file tells the simulation engine what simulations to perform.

Simulation Commands

The simulation engine performs the commands asked for in the execute section of the SimML file using the model defined in the setup section of the same SimML file. Simulation results are reported in another XML file, with a specific section for each command executed. When using the Kanban and Scrum Simulation Visualizer application, the results can also be generated as single page reports similar to webpages.

The current list of execute commands are –

1. *Visual*: A single simulation of the model is performed and the results generated in XML and also viewable in a mimic of a Kanban or Scrum status board.

2. *Monte-carlo*: Multiple simulation runs are performed and the results summarized.

3. *Sensitivity*: Multiple simulations runs are performed and an ordered list of how much each factor in the model influences the output is generated.

4. *Add Staff* (Lean/Kanban only): Multiple simulation runs are performed and suggestions on what Kanban column WIP limits to increase are made.

5. *Forecast Date*: Multiple simulation runs are performed and date and cost forecasts are generated for the model being viewed.

6. *Summary Statistics*: Analyzes actual data and displays summary statistics. This helps decide what probability distribution fits actual real-world data increasing model accuracy.

This chapter covers the basic simulation types mainly used when initially testing and refining a model. The following chapters will look at the forecasting simulations and show how they are used to answer business and staff management problems.

The Execute Section of a SimML File

Sections contained within the execute section of a SimML model tell the simulation engine what actions to perform. You are not limited to a single execution command, the execute section can contain as many commands as you wish to execute, and simulations will be performed in order they are listed.

In addition to being the parent section for simulation commands, the execute section has some attributes of its own that apply across all simulation commands. These attributes default to correct values for most situations, for example, the number of decimal places to report numeric values is three if omitted. These values can be overridden if you need more or less detail in results, or want to specify a subset of backlog deliverables to simulate. Table 7-1 lists all attributes available for the `execute` section.

Table 7-1
Valid attributes of the Execute section.

Attribute	Type	Description
currencyFormat	string (default of C2)	Formatting structure for currency numeric values. C2 is the default, and this uses the local currency symbol and limits the result to 2 decimal places.
dateFormat	string (default of yyyyMMdd)	Formatting structure for date values when reporting and setting values in a model. The default format is yyyyMMdd, which would mean 20110801 for the 1st August 2011. See Appendix B for a full list of format string options.
decimalRounding	integer (default of 3)	The number of decimal places to round numeric values in the results file. Default of 3 if omitted.
deliverables	string	A pipe (|) delimited string of what backlog deliverables to include in simulation. The deliverable names must match exactly those specified in the backlog section of the model. When omitted, all deliverables are simulated.
intervalUnit	days (default), hours	The display unit of simulation intervals (Kanban only). This is the unit that all numeric values in the model are expressed in. Rounding errors on unused time can occur if any unit in the model is < 1, making it good practice to move to hours if any value is less than one day.
limitIntervalsTo	integer (default of 500)	The maximum number of iterations or simulation intervals to perform when attempting to simulate. Simulation stops as soon as all story cards are completed, but if the model is such that it will never finish, or go beyond an expected time, this value avoids being stuck in endless processing. When simulating hours, it may need to be increased if a project is > 2 months.
percentageFormat	string (default of P)	The number format for percentage values in result files.
simulationType	kanban (default), scrum	Determines the project type of Lean/Kanban or Agile/Scrum. Default is Kanban if omitted.

Specifying What Deliverables to Simulate

In chapter 5 we covered how to define the backlog of work to simulate. An optional part of the backlog definition was dividing the work into multiple deliverables. When executing a simulation you can choose all deliverables or a subset of deliverables to be included in the backlog. Listing 7-1 shows how to restrict simulation to just two of the three defined deliverables.

Listing 7-1

Specifying what deliverables to include when simulating.

```
<simulation name="Website Launch">
  <execute deliverables="Must-Haves|Good-To-Haves">
    <visual />
  </execute>

  <setup>
    <backlog type="custom" shuffle="true">
      <deliverable name="Must-Haves">
        <custom … />
      </deliverable>

      <deliverable name="Good-To-Haves">
        <custom … />
      </deliverable>

      <deliverable name="Everything-Remaining">
        <custom … />
      </deliverable>
    </backlog>
```

The value of the `deliverables` string is in the form of a pipe (|) delimited list matching exactly the text in the `name` attribute of the deliverable to be included. The order they are listed is not important.

Limiting the deliverable allows you to forecast multiple scenarios and understand the options of what can go to market earlier than other features in an iterative process. The ability to model a backlog in multiple deliverables helps start the right discussion early with the business stakeholders, helping you manage expectations and putting forward scenarios that get customer value earlier.

Date formats

The format that dates are entered into models and how they are reported is different depending on the geographic region of the user. To allow flexibility in date entry and reporting, it is possible to specify in the model how dates are going to look both in reports and in the model data itself. This is defined as a special formatting string where characters and symbols represent different date and time elements, for example "yyyy" represents the calendar year in 4 digit format. Appendix B shows the extensive set of the string characters and options available, but to help summarize here are some common examples all set to 1st August 2011 –

"yyyyMMdd" - 20110801

"ddMMMyyyy" - 01Aug2011

"yyyy-MMM-dd" - 2011-Aug-01

"dd/MM/yy" - 01/08/11

The default date format is the yyyyMMdd if omitted. Unless simulating in hours and forecasting down to the accuracy of within a day the time format characters (as listed in Appendix B) can be omitted.

Running Simulations using the Kanban and Scrum Visualizer Application

The Kanban and Scrum Visualizer application allows you to edit and execute SimML files. There are only three buttons on the main SimML editing page of the application as shown in Figure 7-1. The buttons labeled Load... and Save... can be used to open and save the current file to and from disk. SimML files are plain text files (in a specific format) and can be edited in any text editor you prefer, and once ready to execute, opened in the Visualizer application by clicking the Load... button and locating that file.

Figure 7-1
Kanban and Scrum Simulation Visualizer application.

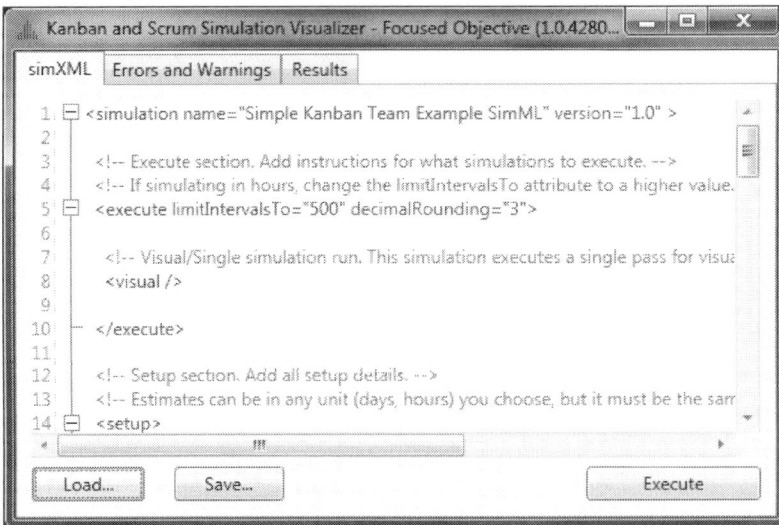

Executing a SimML file is achieved by clicking the Execute button. Once you click on the execute button one of two outcomes will occur. The first is the SimML file executed and returns results which we will cover in a moment; the second outcome is when the file contains an error(s) that inhibit processing.

The second tab in the application window called `Errors and Warnings` shows errors, warnings and informational entries from the attempted SimML file being executed. Figure 7-2 shows the results when an error is encountered during execution. Although there are five informational entries, these do not stop a simulation executing. The single error entry "At least one (execute) sub-element is needed" is an inhibiting error, and this error must be fixed before simulation will begin. There are many error checks that occur before simulation starts. Each error has a description that explains the missing data or formatting problems that need to be fixed. Pay particular attention to upper and lowercase letters in your model attribute names. The SimML file format is case-sensitive and unforgiving.

Figure 7-2
Visualizer application showing what happens when an error is encountered.

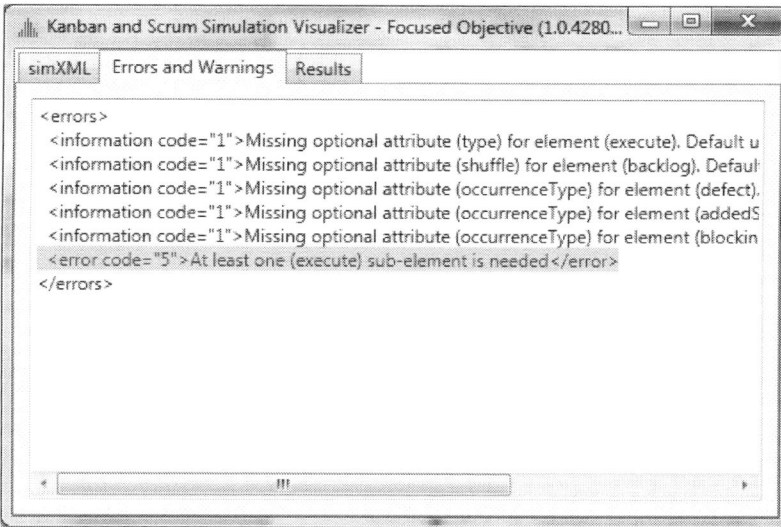

When simulation is successful the results are shown in the Results tab of the main application as shown in Figure 7-3. Although the contents of the results will vary depending on the type of simulation being executed, the results are displayed in a similar fashion as shown in Listing 7-2. Each simulation type's result is embedded within the results section of the file. A section for errors and warnings is added at the end of the file, also as a child section of the simulation section element.

Listing 7-2

The format of the results XML file.

```
<results>
  <[simulation type]> …
  </[simulation type]>
  <[simulation type …]> …
  </[simulation type …]>
  <errors> …
  </errors>
</results>
```

Figure 7-3
Visualizer application showing successful simulation results.

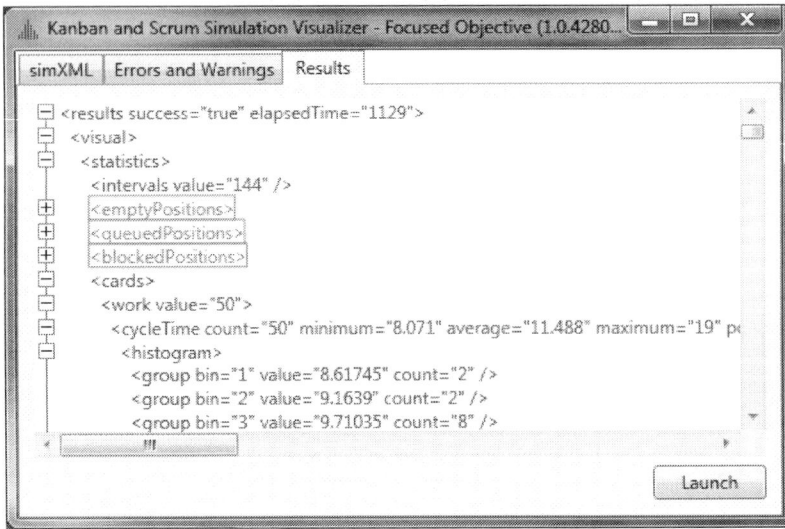

Figure 7-4
HTML Reports are launched from the visualizer application by clicking on the Launch button in the Results tab.

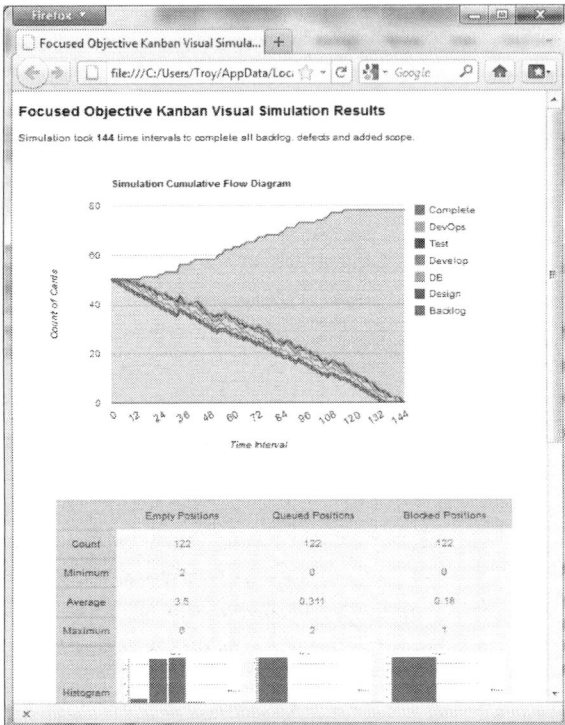

The editors in the visualizer application color-code the section elements and attributes to make them easier to see, and sections can be expanded and collapsed by clicking on the small plus (+) and minus (-) symbols in the left margin. However, even with these conveniences, sometime reports that are easier to read would be appreciated. Clicking on the Launch button of the Results tab launches reports in the web-browser of your choice as shown in Figure 7-4. The resulting reports are different for each simulation type and each will be covered in detail in this chapter and the following chapters.

Visual Simulation

Visual simulation does what its name suggests; it shows one possible visual simulation of the model's results. Its benefits in helping others understand how a Kanban or Scrum status board works, and the impact of defects, added scope and blocking events are immense. When shown a simulation, people grasp the implications of flow (or lack thereof) through either iterations or columns and can relate how they can improve that flow in meaningful ways. Visual simulation doesn't forecast any outcomes; it just shows a simulation of one possible outcome either in the viewer application or generated video file.

Visual simulation is useful -

1. For testing an initial model and refining setup.
2. For visually demonstrating the impact of added scope, defects and blocking events to your team in order to change behavior.
3. For visually demonstrating to your management team the benefits of adding particular resources on a team and project.
4. For seeing the impact of Kanban column WIP limits on un-used and queued (cards completed with no empty positions in the next column) cards.

To execute a Visual simulation, a `visual` section element is added to the execute section of the SimML file. The simplest case is an empty visual XML element in the execute section – `<visual />`. When executing this simulation, a single simulation run is performed, the results added to the Results tab of the visualizer application and either the Kanban Board Viewer or the Scrum Board Viewer is opened.

The Scrum and Kanban Board viewer windows show a digital status board, for example, Figure 7-5 shows a Kanban board. The board represents the model's setup and each iteration or simulation interval can be shown by moving the slider at the bottom of the window from left to right. Story cards moves from the backlog on the left side of the window to complete on the right side of the window. Cards on the board during the current interval are displayed with colored cards. The legend for these card colors are shown above the slider at the bottom of the window. Story cards that are blocked and queued have iconography that can occur on any card type queued (queued is Kanban only status meaning the card is complete but can't move to the next column yet).

Figure 7-5

Kanban Board Viewer shown when using the Visual simulation type. Drag the slider at the bottom of the window to move through time intervals.

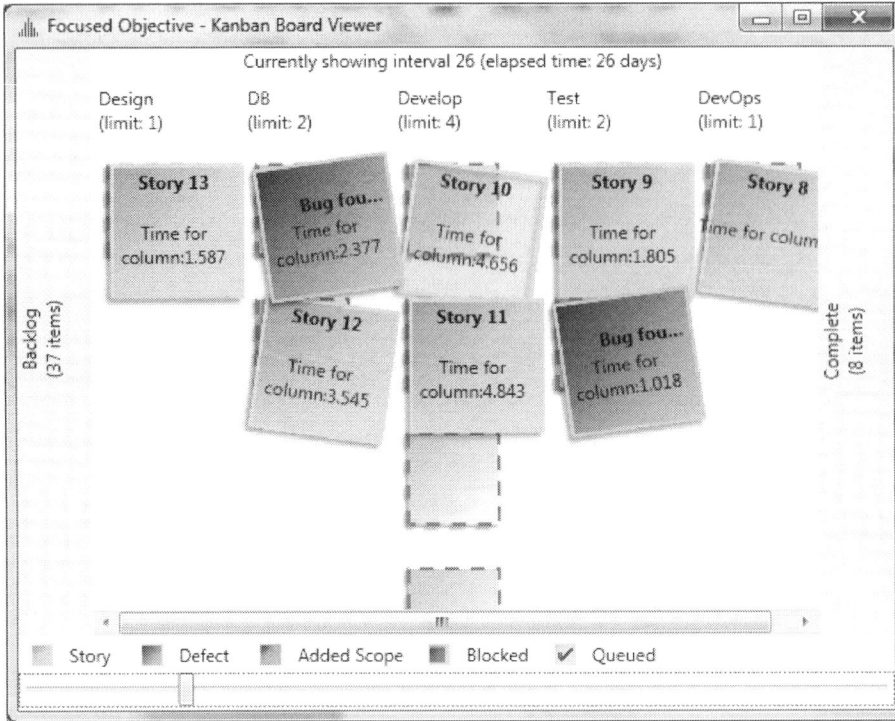

Creating Simulation Videos

To share visual simulation results with other people who don't have the visualizer application installed, a video file can be generated. The format of the video is in a plain AVI file format which can be played by video players, including the Windows Media Player which is shipped by Microsoft in Windows.

Videos are useful for demonstrating the impact of defects, added scope and blocking events to your team during retrospectives. The ability to show the impact visually by running two videos side-by-side with one simulation showing the impact of halving the defect rate, really helps the team understand that every extra bit of effort in re-checking and testing before marking a story card as "done" pays huge dividends. These videos are also useful for demonstrating the impact of adding extra staff members. When people see that upstream work is queued up, and downstream work is under-utilized because one status column has too few resources and WIP limit, you will get the funding for extra staff!

To generate a video of a simulation result, add the attribute `generateVideo="true"` to the visual element –

```
<visual generateVideo="true" />
```

When a model is executed with this element in the execute section, the board viewer is launched, a video produced and then played. Unless told otherwise in the `videoFilename` attribute, the video file is produced into the Windows temporary folder with a random name. A full listing of the attributes allowed in the visual section is shown in Table 7-2.

Table 7-2
The attributes allowed for the Visual execute command.

Attribute	Type	Description
generateVideo	true, false (default)	Determines if a video file is produced of the simulation. When set to true, a video file is created in the windows temporary folder (see sidebar for how to find the temporary folder). Default is false.
videoFramesPerSecond	integer (default of 5)	The number of time intervals or iterations compressed into 1 second of video. Default of 5 if omitted.
videoFilename	string (optional)	The filename the video file is save to after generation. If omitted, the video is saved to the windows temporary directory using a random name. If the visualizer application doesn't have write access to the folder specified, the copy action might fail.

The video file produced is large. There is no compression applied during generation, but there are plenty of tools available for making the file size smaller (google for "compress avi files tools"), including Windows Movie Maker which ships free with Windows XP and Vista, and Windows Live Movie Maker which is available for Windows 7.

> **Sidebar: Finding the Windows Temporary folder**
>
> When files are produced they are placed into the user's temporary folder. To find the location of the temporary folder, open a Windows Explorer application (right-click on the start button in the taskbar and choose Open Windows Explorer), then type %temp% into the address bar and hit enter. Windows Explorer will open the temporary folder for you to browse.

Understanding the Visual Simulation XML Results

The XML results for a visual simulation contain the statistics from a single simulation run. These results are useful when debugging a model because they are fast to produce, however they should not be used for any forecasting. Specific execution commands for forecasting use many hundreds of simulation runs in order to find the most likely patterns in a simulation and these will be covered shortly.

Kanban Visual XML Results

Table 7-3 shows the result XML element structure for a Kanban visual simulation. Sections within the statistics section use the statistical summary format described in Chapter 3 - Interpreting Simulation Results Summary Statistics. This includes the standard summary statistics and histograms of the measurement being reported. The other sections that don't use this structure are `intervals`, which reports the single number of simulation intervals (hours or days, whatever you configured in the model) to completely exhaust backlog; and the `cumulativeFlow` section. The cumulative flow section provides raw data that can be used in other applications for further analysis. A cumulative flow diagram reports the number of cards in each status column for each time interval. The errors, warnings and informational entries are added in a section called `errors` at the bottom of the file. If you performed a successful simulation, this section will just contain warnings and information errors – most commonly the simulation engine reporting what values it used for optional attributes that were omitted from the model.

Table 7-3

Visual simulation results XML structure for Kanban simulation.

Element	Description
\<results\>	Root element for all results.
\<visual ...\>	Beginning of the visual results section.
\<statistics\>	Beginning of statistic results section
\<intervals ... /\>	The number of intervals to complete simulation.
\<emptyPositions ... /\>	The number of empty (un-filled) card positions during simulation intervals.
\<queuedPositions ... /\>	The number of queued (complete but no available position in next column) card positions during simulation intervals.
\<blockedPositions ... /\>	The number of blocked cards during simulation intervals.
\<cards\>	Beginning of the card statistics section.
\<work ... /\>	The count and cycle-time statistics of work cards.
\<addedScope ... /\>	The count and cycle-time statistics of added scope cards.
\<defect ... /\>	The count and cycle-time statistics of defect cards.
\</cards\>	End of the card statistics section.
\</statistics\>	End of the statistic results section.
\<cumulativeFlow\>	Beginning of the cumulative flow section.
\<data ... /\>	Cumulative flow data in Comma-Separated-Value format (CSV) that can be copied using the clipboard into other applications (like Microsoft Excel) for further analysis.
\<chart ... /\>	Cumulative flow data in Javascript form. This form of data can be used to build interactive charts in HTML file reports. Results are exposed as pre-populated Javascript arrays that can be coded against.
\</cumulativeFlow\>	End of the cumulative flow section.
\</visual\>	End of the visual results section.
\<errors\>	Beginning of the errors section.
\<error| information| warning ...\/\>	One or more errors, warnings or information section elements describing the issues with the currently executed SimML model.
\</errors\>	End of the errors section.
\</results\>	End of the results section.

Scrum Visual XML Results

Table 7-4 shows the result XML element structure for a Scrum visual simulation. Sections within the statistics section use the statistical summary format described in Chapter 3 -

Interpreting Simulation Results Summary Statistics. This includes the standard summary statistics and histograms of the measurement being reported. The only section that doesn't use this structure is `iterations`, which reports the single number of simulation iterations taken to completely exhaust backlog. The errors, warnings and informational entries are added in a section called `errors` at the bottom of the file. If you performed a successful simulation, this section will just contain warnings and information errors – most commonly the simulation engine reporting what values it used for optional attributes that were omitted from the model.

Table 7-4
Visual simulation results XML structure for Scrum simulation.

Element	Description
****	Root element for all results.
<visual ...>	Beginning of the visual results section.
<statistics>	Beginning of statistic results section
<iterations ... />	The number of iterations to complete simulation.
<pointsAllocatedPer-Iteration ... />	The points allocated per iteration statistics for all iterations.
<cards>	Beginning of the card statistics section.
<work ... />	The count and point-size statistics of work cards.
<addedScope ... />	The count and point-size statistics of added scope cards.
<defect ... />	The count and point-size statistics of defect cards.
</cards>	End of the card statistics section.
</statistics>	End of the statistic results section.
</visual>	End of the visual results section.
<errors>	Beginning of the errors section.
<error| information| warning ...>	One or more errors, warnings or information section elements describing the issues with the currently executed SimML model.
</errors>	End of the errors section.
****	End of the results section.

Monte-carlo Simulation

Monte-carlo simulation performs many simulation passes over the same model and summarizes the results. By performing more simulation passes that each use different random-numbers for values (but within the bounds you specified) the more likely outcomes become obvious when analyzing the results.

Monte-carlo simulation is an important building block for the more targeted simulation execution commands like `forecastDate`, `sensitivity` and `addStaff`. You shouldn't find yourself running a monte-carlo simulation until you are an advanced user and drilling into a model to understand how the more feature rich simulations got the answer they did.

The monte-carlo simulation command has a single attribute – `cycles`, which specifies how many simulation runs to summarize. For example, Listing 7-3 performs a Monte-carlo simulation of 250 cycles.

Listing 7-3

Executing a Monte-carlo simulation of 250 cycles.

```
<simulation name="Example SimML">
  <execute>
    <monteCarlo cycles="250" />
  </execute>
  <setup>
    ...
  </setup>
</simulation>
```

The XML results are almost identical to the visual commands results, except that the `pointsPerIteration` and the `intervals` section are summary statistic structures (see Chapter 3) because rather than the value from a single run, they are now summaries of multiple runs.

When choosing the number of cycles to execute, remember that the more cycles the longer it takes to perform simulation and the more computer memory is used. Best practice is to start low (less than 50) until you are happy with the model and then increase it to hundreds to get more samples. The more samples you have the more pronounced any pattern in the histograms (remember the Central Limit Theorem in Chapter 3)

There is no visual viewer for Monte-carlo simulations, the results are generated in XML format (Figure 7-6), and if the Launch button is clicked on the results tab of the Kanban and Scrum Visualizer application, a HTML report is generated (Figure 7-7).

Figure 7-6
XML Results for a Monte-carlo simulation.

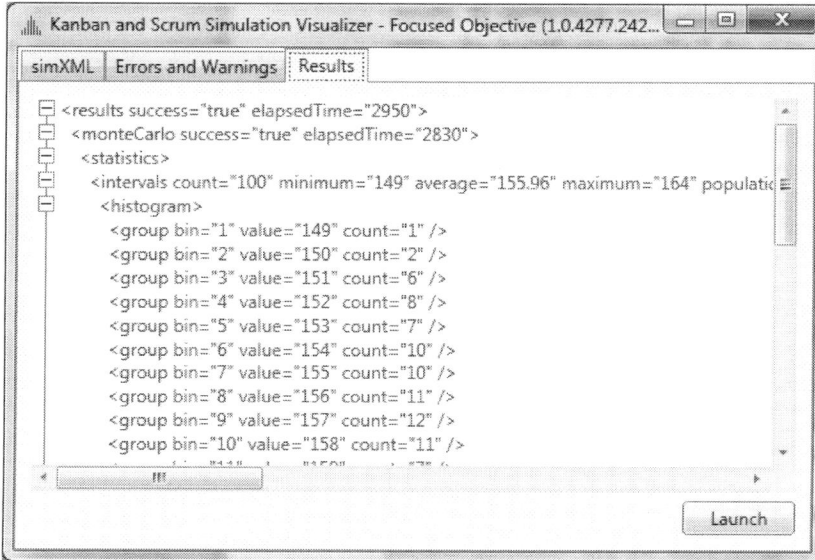

Figure 7-7
HTML Results for Monte-carlo simulation.

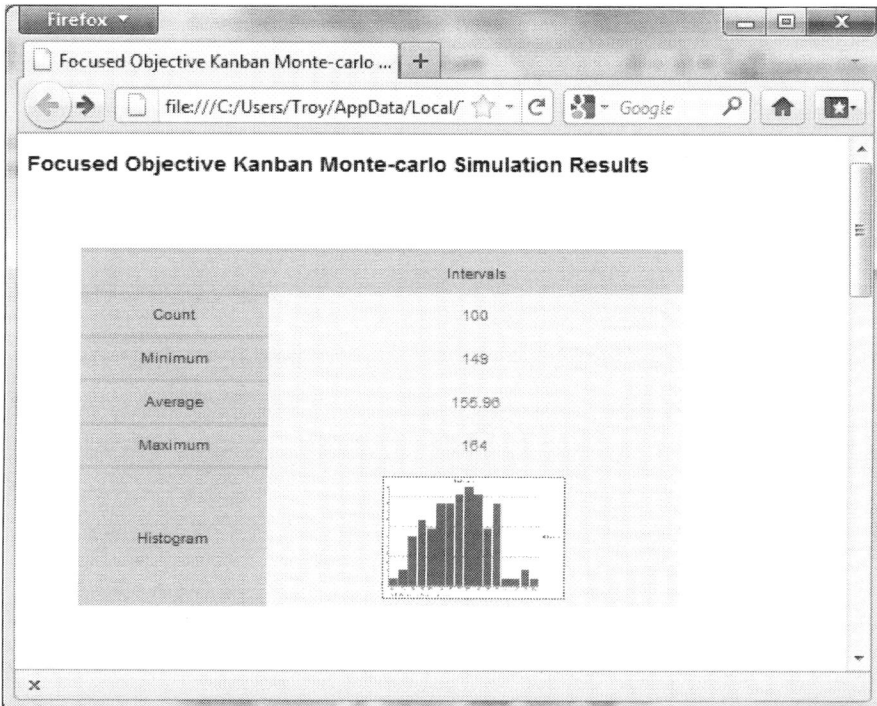

The most important part of the Monte-carlo results is the histogram of intervals for Lean/Kanban or iterations for Agile/Scrum. These histograms represent the pattern of how much time is required to complete the entire backlog and events. For example, consider the following results from a Kanban Monte-carlo simulation -

```
<results success="true" elapsedTime="2590">
  <monteCarlo success="true" elapsedTime="2585">
    <statistics>
      <intervals count="100"
      minimum="147" average="156.83" maximum="165"
      populationStandardDeviation="3.766"
      sampleStandardDeviation="3.785"
      median="157" mode="157"
      fifthPercentile="151" twentyFifthPercentile="154"
      seventyFifthPercentile="159" ninetyFifthPercentile="163">
```

These results are indicating that the 90th percentile range is from 151 days to 163 days (the fifthPercentile to the ninetyFifthPercentile). Over a 6 month project, a little over 2 weeks is an acceptable narrow range in which to forecast. You have to decide what level of confidence you are willing to present to others – my advice is the 95th percentile value, but never below the mode value. Remember though, the forecastDate simulation command carries out more analysis and considers more factors that move from raw iterations and intervals into a calendar date – if you are using the Monte-carlo results in raw form, take care!

Summary

This chapter has introduced the Kanban and Scrim Visualizer application and demonstrated how to execute two of the many simulation commands – Visual and Monte-carlo. The following chapters look at the more sophisticated simulation commands that help building date and cost forecasts and understanding of the factors most influencing a simulation model's result.

Chapter 8
Forecasting Dates and Cost

Forecasting probable release dates and costs is the main end-game of simulation. Combining the power of an event driven simulation engine that properly incorporates the flow-on effect of those events on project completion time with Monte-carlo analysis, the Focused Objective simulation engine will resolve accurate forecasts. In Chapter 7 we saw how to execute a Monte-carlo simulation manually. This will return the number of simulation intervals or the number of iterations to move the entire backlog, defects and added-scope from started to the completed list. Knowing the intervals or iterations allows a calendar date to be calculated. This is the basis of forecasting.

Performing Forecast Date Simulations

The `forecastDate` command gives the percentage likelihood and the completion dates from the simulation run summaries of a model. You have the options of choosing the days of the week that work takes place, the starting date and any days that shouldn't be counted (public holidays for example). Once the models are simulating correctly using the `visual` command, it's time to execute the `forecastDate` command. Forecasting before checking your model with a visual simulation is risky and should be avoided.

There are slight differences between Agile/Scrum simulation and Lean/Kanban `forecastDate` simulation. The differences are in how work days are calculated from simulation results. Kanban simulation converts *simulation intervals* into work days, while Scrum simulation converts *iterations* to work days. Once days are calculated, work days from the start date are enumerated until a completion date is reached.

Listing 8-1 shows how to execute a forecast date simulation for a Kanban project. The `intervalsToOneDay` attribute is used to convert simulation intervals to days. If the model values have been expressed in days, set this value to 1; if the model has been expressed in hours, set this value to 8 (or if needed, use 6 to account for lunch breaks, meetings and other down-time during a day).

Listing 8-1

Forecast Date simulation for Kanban model.

```
<simulation name="Forecast Date Kanban Sample">
   <execute dateFormat="ddMMMyyyy">
      <forecastDate cycles="250" intervalsToOneDay="1"
        startDate="01Aug2011"
        workDays="monday,tuesday,wednesday,thursday,friday"
        costPerDay="800.00" />
```

```
  </execute>
  <setup>
    ...
  </setup>
</simulation>
```

The `forecastDate` section has other important attributes. The `startDate` is obvious, and needs to be in the format described in the execute section (`dateFormat`, see Appendix B). This is the first workday when counting towards completion. You specify what days of the week are work days. The default if the `workDays` attribute is omitted is Monday to Friday, but you can choose as many or as few that are available. Each day of the week name must be separated by a comma (,) character.

Another attribute is the `costPerDay` value. This per-day cost is multiplied by the number of work-days calculated to complete the project. How the value entered in the `costPerDay` attribute is computed is up to you. For the examples used earlier in Chapter 2 of this book, I calculated the number of staff and estimated a per-day fixed cost for them by the simple estimate ($100K / 52 / 5) x number of staff. Make sure that you keep this value up-to-date when simulating the impact of adding or removing staff. By using the `costPerDay` to forecast costs it is easy to see the impact of adding staff and finishing earlier versus reducing staff and finishing later.

Listing 8-2 shows how to execute a `forecastDate` command for a Scrum project. Rather than specifying how to convert intervals to one day, you specify the number of days per Agile/Scrum iteration. The `workDaysPerIteration` attribute is the number of workdays each iteration. There is no standard number of days for an Agile or Scrum project iteration size, but 10 days is common (2 weeks). The other attributes are identical to those mentioned earlier in the Lean/Kanban forecast date example.

Listing 8-2
Forecast Date simulation for Scrum model.

```
<simulation name="Scrum Team SimML File" >
  <execute type="Scrum" dateFormat="ddMMMyyyy">
    <forecastDate cycles="250" workDaysPerIteration="10"
    startDate="01Aug2011"
    workDays="monday,tuesday,wednesday,thursday,friday"
    costPerDay="800.00" />
  </execute>
  <setup>
    ...
  </setup>
</simulation>
```

Table 8-1 documents all of the available attributes of the `forecastDate` section. The mandatory attributes are `cycles` and `startDate`.

Table 8-1

All available attributes for the forecastDate section.

Attribute	Type	Description
costPerDay	number	The cost per work day used for calculating the total cost for each forecast date.
cycles	integer (mandatory)	The number of simulation iterations performed as part of this simulation. Must be > 0.
intervalsToOneDay	integer (default of 1)	The number of simulation intervals that equals one work day for Kanban models. Use 1 if the model estimate units are expressed in days, or 8 if the model is expressed in hours (or 6 to account for down-time).
startDate	date (mandatory)	The first work day of the project. Days will be forecasted from this date as day 1 forwards until all workdays are complete. The format of the date must take the format in the execute section, or one of the following formats: "yyyyMMdd", "yyyyMd", "yyyy-MM-dd", "yyyy-M-d", "yyyy/MM/dd" (see Appendix B)
workDays	string (defaults Monday to Friday)	Comma separated list of week day names that are work days. Defaults to "Monday,Tuesday,Wednesday,Thursday,Friday" if omitted.
workDaysPerIteration	integer (default of 10)	The number of work days per iteration for Scrum projects. Defaults to 10 if omitted.

Understanding the Forecast Date Results XML

The result from a `forecastDate` simulation is a list of dates, likelihood percentage and cost for every possible outcome. A possible outcome is a result uncovered at least one simulation cycle.

The result XML file (an example is shown in Listing 8-3) has a section for the specific results of the forecast date simulation, called `forecastDate`. The input attributes are repeated for convenience. The actual forecasts are a series of date sections in a dates parent section. Each entry will have the number of intervals (for Kanban) or iterations (for Scrum), and then a date. The date will be formatted as the `dateFormat` attribute in the execute section has defined.

Each entry will also have a likelihood value as a percentage. 100% means that every simulation performed completed by equal-to or less than this date, and 0% means that no simulation completed by the given date. Each date will be in ascending order, with the most likely dates appearing later in the list. It is up to you to choose the date that matches your appetite for risk. 95% is a common value. Simulations occurring above this range are often outliers, but possible outcomes given your model. If you are worrying about the last 5%, you must be very confident in your model; so I suggest using the 95% value (or nearest to that) and putting your effort into making sure the model is as valid as possible.

Cost for each date is calculated by multiplying your `costPerDay` attribute value (in the `forecastDate` section) by the number of work days calculated for each simulation possibility. This cost calculation is to allow comparing different team sizes and delivery date options. Although it is accurately calculated from the model, you should consider adding other costs for hardware, hosting, marketing, furniture, etc. to get a complete picture of project costs if that level of detail is important.

Listing 8-3 shows the results from a Scrum `forecastDate` simulation. Agile processes deliver in fixed iteration sizes. The results show a list of iterations that at least one simulation found a solution, up to the number of iterations to completion that every simulation was equal-to or less than. Work days was calculated from the number of iterations using the formula: `iterations * workDaysPerIteration`, and cost was calculated as: `workDays * costPerWorkDay`.

Listing 8-3

Results of a forecastDate simulation on a Scrum project.

```
<results success="true" elapsedTime="454">
  <forecastDate startDate="01Aug2011" workDaysPerIteration="10"
          workdays="monday,tuesday,wednesday,thursday,friday"
          costPerDay="800" >
    <dates>
      <date iterations="9" workDays="90" date="03Dec2011"
          likelihood="3.00 %" cost="$72,000.00" />
      <date iterations="10" workDays="100" date="17Dec2011"
          likelihood="28.00 %" cost="$80,000.00" />
      <date iterations="11" workDays="110" date="31Dec2011"
          likelihood="65.00 %" cost="$88,000.00" />
      <date iterations="12" workDays="120" date="14Jan2012"
          likelihood="94.00 %" cost="$96,000.00" />
      <date iterations="13" workDays="130" date="28Jan2012"
          likelihood="100.00 %" cost="$104,000.00" />
    </dates>
  </forecastDate>
  <errors>
...
  </errors>
</results>
```

Listing 8-4 shows the `forecastDate` results for a Kanban project. Instead of agile iterations being the basis for work days, simulation intervals are used. To recap, Kanban models can use estimates in any time unit of measure you choose, you just have to be consistent. During simulation, 1 unit of simulation time is incremented each simulation interval whether it is in hours or days. It's not until we want to convert this unit to a date that it is necessary to know how many simulation intervals equal one day, and this is specified in the `intervalsToOneDay` attribute of the `forecastDate` command. Work days is calculated with the formula: `intervals / intervalsToOneDay`, and cost is calculated as: `workDays * costPerDay`.

Listing 8-4

Results of a forecastDate simulation on a Kanban project.

```
<results success="true" elapsedTime="976">
```

```
<forecastDate startDate="01Aug2011" intervalsToOneDay="1"
    workdays="monday,tuesday,wednesday,thursday,friday"
    costPerDay="800" >
  <dates>
    <date intervals="47" workDays="47" date="05Oct2011"
        likelihood="2.00 %" cost="$37,600.00" />
    <date intervals="48" workDays="48" date="06Oct2011"
        likelihood="5.00 %" cost="$38,400.00" />
    <date intervals="49" workDays="49" date="07Oct2011"
        likelihood="16.00 %" cost="$39,200.00" />
    <date intervals="50" workDays="50" date="08Oct2011"
        likelihood="29.00 %" cost="$40,000.00" />
    <date intervals="51" workDays="51" date="11Oct2011"
        likelihood="45.00 %" cost="$40,800.00" />
    <date intervals="52" workDays="52" date="12Oct2011"
        likelihood="57.00 %" cost="$41,600.00" />
    <date intervals="53" workDays="53" date="13Oct2011"
        likelihood="74.00 %" cost="$42,400.00" />
    <date intervals="54" workDays="54" date="14Oct2011"
        likelihood="92.00 %" cost="$43,200.00" />
    <date intervals="55" workDays="55" date="15Oct2011"
        likelihood="99.00 %" cost="$44,000.00" />
    <date intervals="56" workDays="56" date="18Oct2011"
        likelihood="100.00 %" cost="$44,800.00" />
  </dates>
</forecastDate>
<errors>
...
</errors>
</results>
```

Excluding Dates from Workdays

Both Kanban and Scrum forecasts count a number of workdays from the starting date. Non-work days are skipped (those days not listed in the `workDays` attribute). It is possible to list other dates to exclude to account for public holidays, training, or other days where work will not proceed that day.

Listing 8-5 demonstrates how to exclude the federal 2012 holidays in the US from being counted as work days during a date forecast. The format used is one or more `exclude` sections within a parent `excludes` element. The format of the date should match that listed in the `dateFormat` attribute of the execute section.

Listing 8-5

Excluding dates from the forecastDate date calculations.

```
<simulation name="Skip Holidays Example">
  <execute dateFormat="ddMMMyyyy" >
    <forecastDate cycles="250"  intervalsToOneDay="1"
        startDate="01Jan2011"
        workDays="monday,tuesday,wednesday,thursday,friday"
```

```
            costPerDay="800.00">
              <excludes>
                <exclude date="02Jan2012">New Years Day</exclude>
                <exclude date="16Jan2012">
                    Birthday of Martin Luther King, Jr.</exclude>
                <exclude date="20Feb2012">
                    Washington's Birthday</exclude>
                <exclude date="28May2012">Memorial Day</exclude>
                <exclude date="04Jul2012">Independence Day</exclude>
                <exclude date="03Sep2012">Labor Day</exclude>
                <exclude date="08Oct2012">Columbus Day</exclude>
                <exclude date="12Nov2012">Veterans Day</exclude>
                <exclude date="22Nov2012">Thanksgiving Day</exclude>
                <exclude date="25Dec2012">Christmas Day</exclude>
          </excludes>
      </forecastDate>
  </execute>
  <setup>
...
  </setup>
</simulation>
```

For convenience, and the ability to manage excluded dates in an external file is available to reduce duplication and errors. Listing 8-6 shows how to include the contents of another file within a SimML file (although we are using it here for the excludes section, any section can be external). The file referenced in this case has the US Federal holidays for 2012, and its contents are shown in Listing 8-7. The folder and filename must be the fully qualified path and file name of the file, and the logged-in user must have permissions to that folder and file. If the file is not found, an error is reported.

Listing 8-6

Using include file to manage public holiday dates in a separate file

```
<simulation name="Skip Holidays Example">
   <execute dateFormat="ddMMMyyyy" >
      <forecastDate cycles="250"  intervalsToOneDay="1"
    startDate="01Jan2011"
    workDays="monday,tuesday,wednesday,thursday,friday"
    costPerDay="800.00">
        <?include
source="c:\users\...\Documents\2012_US_Holidays.xml" ?>
    </forecastDate>
  </execute>
  <setup>
...
  </setup>
</simulation>
```

Listing 8-7

The contents of the "2012_US_Holidays.xml" file

```
<excludes>
  <!-- Federal US Holidays -->
  <exclude date="02Jan2012">New Years Day</exclude>
  <exclude date="16Jan2012">
     Birthday of Martin Luther King, Jr.</exclude>
  <exclude date="20Feb2012">Washington's Birthday</exclude>
  <exclude date="28May2012">Memorial Day</exclude>
  <exclude date="04Jul2012">Independence Day</exclude>
  <exclude date="03Sep2012">Labor Day</exclude>
  <exclude date="08Oct2012">Columbus Day</exclude>
  <exclude date="12Nov2012">Veterans Day</exclude>
  <exclude date="22Nov2012">Thanksgiving Day</exclude>
  <exclude date="25Dec2012">Christmas Day</exclude>
</excludes>
```

Summary

This chapter shows how to forecast the completion date for a model. This is one of the most powerful simulation commands you will execute when making date and cost predictions. It will be ran many times when performing what-if experiments on the model to understand the impact various events and team configurations.

The next chapter examines how to use simulation to understand the impact of different staff resourcing options for a project, and answering the common question "What skills does my next hire need?"

Chapter 9
Analyzing Staff and WIP Limits

Kanban models can be analyzed to determine the impact of increasing the amount of concurrent work for each column has on various measures (time to complete a project, story cycle-time, etc). Often columns represent a different staff skill expertise, and by understanding what work in process (WIP) limits to increase, you know what is the next best staff hire. Although there are some future plans, Scrum projects don't contain the staff expertise in their model and can't be analyzed this way.

Staff Planning and WIP Limits

During the planning phase before a project starts it is important to understand the impact of various WIP limits and the staff required to do the work on completing cards in those positions on the board. Initially, I use a staff to WIP limit ratio of 1:1 to find the right board balance, and then increase this ratio to 2 WIP limit positions per staff member in the columns where blocking events are likely (no need leaving a person idle!).

Visually simulating a model makes it easy to see whether some columns have excessive queuing (completed cards with no open position to their right), or empty board positions (unfilled positions). Both of these Lean flow problems impact cycle-time and the total number of Intervals to complete a project. The add staff simulation quickly shows the best balance of WIP limits across the entire Kanban board, and demonstrates why certain staff configurations have the most impact on delivery forecasts.

In an ongoing project, it is important to be able to answer the following question when asked by your boss – "What staff do you need to deliver your project earlier?" The reflex most managers have is to throw more developers at a project, but I find that due to constraints in other resource expertise (QA, Design, DevOps), the project timeline impact of those hires are minimal. The add staff simulation gives solid data and advice on what resources have the most impact on reducing a date forecast. Once new WIP limits have been decided, performing a `forecastDate` with the new column configuration will show the new completion date.

This chapter covers how to execute an add staff simulations and how to interpret those results.

Performing Add Staff Simulations

Listing 9-1 shows how to execute an `addStaff` command. This example will find the next five column WIP limit suggestions that most decrease the number of simulation intervals (leading to an earlier delivery date).

Listing 9-1

Add Staff analysis command. This example makes five WIP limit increase suggestions that most decrease the number of simulation intervals.

```
<simulation name="Add Staff Example" >
  <execute>
    <addStaff
        cycles="50" count = "5" optimizeForLowest="intervals"  />
  </execute>
  <setup>
  ...
  </setup>
</simulation>
```

Table 9-1 documents all of the available attributes of the `addStaff` section. The cycles attribute defines how many simulation cycles are averaged when performing an analysis. The more cycles specified the longer simulation will take to perform. Keeping this value below 100 is recommended unless you see very small changes in the value being optimized and think more samples might give a clearer winner. As a guide, adding 5 staff to a 5 column Kanban board will take over 1 minute with a setting of 50 cycles.

The `count` attribute is the number of WIP limit change recommendations to find during simulation. The count is normally a positive number to find staff additions, but it can be negative when minimizing cycle-time, a special case covered later in this chapter. The value of count solely determines how many suggestions are made; it doesn't influence the analysis and suggestion process in any way - just how often it runs.

The `optimizeForLowest` is the main attribute to consider carefully. It specifies the result value that is being minimized. For example, the default is simulation intervals; The WIP limit increase that results in the lowest number of intervals to complete will be the suggestion made by the `addStaff` command. The other options of minimizing the number of queued positions, empty positions or queued and empty positions are available but rarely offer insights that aren't catered for by the other options. Optimizing cycle-time is the other common value, and this is covered separately later in this chapter.

Table 9-1

All available attributes for the addStaff section.

Attribute	Type	Description
count	integer (default of 1)	The number of WIP limit's to increase. A full cycle of simulation will occur for each WIP analysis.
cycles	integer (mandatory)	The number of simulation iterations performed as part of this simulation. Must be > 0.

optimizeForLowest	intervals (default), cycleTime, queued, empty, queuedAndEmpty	The result value to minimize. For example, if "intervals" are chosen, each analysis will find the simulation solution with the lowest number of simulation intervals. The default is intervals if omitted.

Limiting the Columns Recommended

The `addStaff` command analyzes all columns unless you specify the subset of columns to analyze. You may exclude some columns because it is known in advance that hiring a certain skill expertise isn't going to be possible, or you know that the current need isn't the same as the long term need.

To restrict analysis to a subset of columns, two or more column sections can be added to the `addStaff` section. Each column section needs an id value that matches the column id value of the columns defined in the setup section. Also, the maximum WIP limit allowed to be reached is specified. For example, if `maxWip="10"` is specified, then only changes that keep the WIP Limit in the specified column to 10 or under are considered. This can be used to inhibit a column taking more resources than you can fulfill whilst starving other columns from analysis.

Listing 9-2 shows how to execute an `addStaff` command that only searches three of the five columns.

Listing 9-2

Add Staff example with restricted columns. Only columns listed will be analyzed (Design, DB and Test).

```
<simulation name="Add Staff Example" >
  <execute>
    <addStaff count = "5" optimizeForLowest="intervals"
            cycles="50" >
       <column id="1" maxWip="10" />
       <column id="2" maxWip="10" />
       <column id="4" maxWip="10" />
    </addStaff>
  </execute>
  <setup>
    <columns>
      <column id="1" estimateLowBound="1" estimateHighBound="2"
            wipLimit="1">Design</column>
      <column id="2" estimateLowBound="2" estimateHighBound="4"
            wipLimit="2">DB</column>
      <column id="3" estimateLowBound="1" estimateHighBound="5"
            wipLimit="4">Develop</column>
      <column id="4" estimateLowBound="1" estimateHighBound="2"
            wipLimit="2">Test</column>
      <column id="5" estimateLowBound="1" estimateHighBound="1"
            wipLimit="1">DevOps</column>
    </columns>
    ...
```

```
    </setup>
</simulation>
```

Understanding the Add Staff Analysis Results

The results from an add staff analysis is a set of column WIP limit suggestions, either an increase or decrease. Table 9-2 shows the result XML element structure for an Add Staff simulation, and an example section is shown in Listing 9-3.

Table 9-2

Add Staff simulation results XML structure for Kanban simulation.

Element	Description
	Root element for all results.
<addStaff ...>	Beginning of the addStaff results section.
<wipSuggestion ...>	Beginning of one or more wipSuggestion sections
<original ... />	The simulation statistics before the change was made.
<new ... />	The simulation statistics after the change was made.
</wipSuggestion>	End of the wipSuggestion section.
... more ...	More wipSuggestion sections...
</addStaff>	End of the addStaff results section.
<errors>	Beginning of the errors section.
<error| information| warning .../>	One or more errors, warnings or information section elements describing the issues with the currently executed SimML model.
</errors>	End of the errors section.
	End of the results section.

Listing 9-3

A single wipSuggestion section.

```
    <wipSuggestion columnId="2" columnName="DB"
                   originalWip="2" newWip="3"
                   intervalImprovement="11.92"
                   cycleTimeImprovement="1.26"
                   emptyPositionsImprovement="0.12"
                   queuedPositionsImprovement="11.19"
                   queuedAndEmptyPositionsImprovement="0.87">
        <original>
            <statistics>
                ...
            </statistics>
        </original>
        <new>
            <statistics>
                ...
```

```
      </statistics>
    </new>
  </wipSuggestion>
```

If more than one suggestion is made (meaning the count attribute for the `addStaff` command is greater than 1), there will be multiple `wipSuggestion` sections in the results. The recommendations are cumulative, meaning that the second suggestion assumes the first suggestion has been made and so on. For each suggestion the data shown in Table 9-3 is reported. In addition, the full simulation statistics of the original model and the new model is added to the suggestion for further manual analysis (by deeply curious people).

Table 9-3
wipSuggestion result attribute reference.

Attribute	Description
columnId	The column id for this suggestion. Matches the id specified in the setup/columns section of the model.
columnName	The column name for this suggestion. Looked up from the name specified for the column in the setup/columns section of the model.
originalWip	The original Wip limit currently specified. This will be the wip limit specified in the setup/columns section unless this column has been suggested previously in these results. Results are cumulative, meaning that the next suggestion assumes that all previous suggested have been made (their WIP limit increased on the columns they specify).
newWip	The new Wip limit suggested.
intervalImprovement	The number of intervals reduced with this Wip suggestion. Calculated by: original intervals - new intervals. A larger positive number is better. A negative result means that the suggestion makes the project longer.
cycleTimeImprovement	The cycle-time reduction with this Wip suggestion. Calculated by: original cycle-time - new cycle-time. A negative result means that the suggestion makes the cycle-time longer. Only work cards cycle-time is considered.
emptyPositionsImprovement	The number of empty positions reduced with this Wip suggestion. Calculated by: original empty positions - new empty positions. A larger positive number is better. A negative result means that the suggestion causes more empty positions.
queuedPositionsImprovement	The number of queued positions reduced with this Wip suggestion. Calculated by: original queued positions - new queued positions. A larger positive number is better. A negative result means that the suggestion causes more queued positions.

There is a lot of data in these results, but the most important are the attributes in each `wipSuggestion` section itself. These attributes describe the column and the delta of improvements (or worsening from the result measures that are not being optimized) over the original model. A quick way to interpret the results is to launch the HTML report by clicking on the launch button on the results tab of the Kanban and Scrum Visualizer application as shown in Figure 9-1.

Figure 9-1

The Visualizer application showing addStaff results. Click on the Launch button to see the results in HTML

The HTML report for an Add Staff analysis has two sections. The upper section is a set of mini-charts (see Figure 9-2) showing the improvement or worsening after each recommendation is made. Clicking on any of the four charts maximizes it in the browser window. The lower section is a table that documents the recommendation and improvements in numerical form (see Figure 9-3).

Figure 9-2

The addStaff HTML report chart section. Clicking on each chart maximizes it.

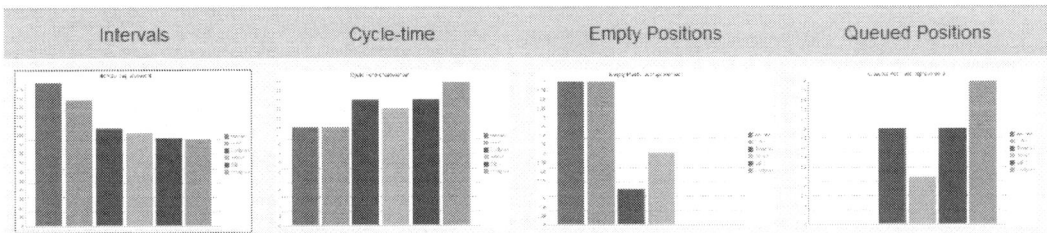

The charts shown in Figure 9-2 allow a quick visual analysis of each suggestions impact on the four measures. For this example, the Add Staff was optimizing for the lowest number of intervals, as charted by the left-most chart. Even at the low zoom level, you can see that the first two suggestions have the greatest impact, and the subsequent three less so. You can also see the second chart shows work card cycle-time is negatively impacted by increasing work in progress, proof that the Kanban process books are correct: more work in process generally means higher cycle-times. If you are trying to reduce cycle-time, a specific section in this chapter addresses how to model and simulate for that goal.

Figure 9-3 shows the results in tabular data form. Each suggestion is a column in the table, with that suggestions specific data in the rows below. I know I've said it previously, but it can't be stressed enough that these suggestions are cumulative (notice how the original WIP is incremented in subsequent suggestions for the same Kanban column), and the improvement is over the original baseline simulation results - not the previous suggestion.

Figure 9-3
The addStaff HTML table section. Remember: All improvements are cumulative and calculated over the original baseline result.

Increase WIP in Column	DB	Design	Test	DB	Design
Original wip	2	1	2	3	2
New wip	3	2	3	4	3
Interval improvement	11.92%	31.96%	34.71%	38.53%	39.34%
Cycle-time improvement	1.26%	-20.44%	-14.46%	-26.67%	-38.99%
Empty positions improvement	0.12%	80.92%	53.73%	89.56%	93.68%
Queued positions improvement	11.19%	-505.72%	-398.47%	-773.16%	-1162.93%
Queued & Empty positions improvement	0.87%	41.31%	23.2%	31.31%	8.83%

Reducing Cycle-Time Simulation

You may want to reduce the cycle-time of moving work through a Kanban process in order to deliver pieces of functionality to production earlier and with more predictability, rather than a large number of features with wide delivery variance.

The count attribute for the `addStaff` command can be positive or negative. When negative, WIP limits are analyzed for removal, decremented during analysis. To analyze a model and see what WIP limits could be reduced to most impact cycle-time, set the count attribute to a negative number and `optimizeForLowest="cycleTime"`, for example -

```
<addStaff count = "-5" optimizeForLowest="cycleTime" cycles="50"/>
```

The result suggestions reduce column WIP Limits looking for the changes that reduce cycle-time. To decrease cycle-time on a Kanban board, there has to be significant queuing in earlier columns either due to WIP limit constraints in columns to the right, or events that delay completion of work (defects, blocking events or added scope). Listing 9-4 shows an example where Column 3 is the choke-point for cards moving through Columns 1 and 2. The results of this simple test are shown in Figure 9-4, and suggest to reduce Column 1's WIP limit to 1 (leave work in the backlog rather than start the cycle-time clock and immediately queue that work).

Listing 9-4

Example add staff simulation that will reduce wip limits to minimize cycle-time.

```
<simulation name="Cycle time reduction" >
  <execute>
   <addStaff cycles="50" count="-3" optimizeForLowest="cycleTime"/>
  </execute>
  <setup>
    <backlog type="simple" simpleCount="50" />
    <columns>
        <column id="1" wipLimit="4"
            estimateLowBound="1" estimateHighBound="1">
            Column 1</column>
        <column id="2" wipLimit="3"
            estimateLowBound="1" estimateHighBound="1">
            Column 2</column>
        <column id="3" wipLimit="1"
            estimateLowBound="1" estimateHighBound="1">
            Column 3</column>
        </columns>
    </setup>
</simulation>
```

Figure 9-4
Results of the add staff simulation looking to decrease cycle-time by decreasing WIP.

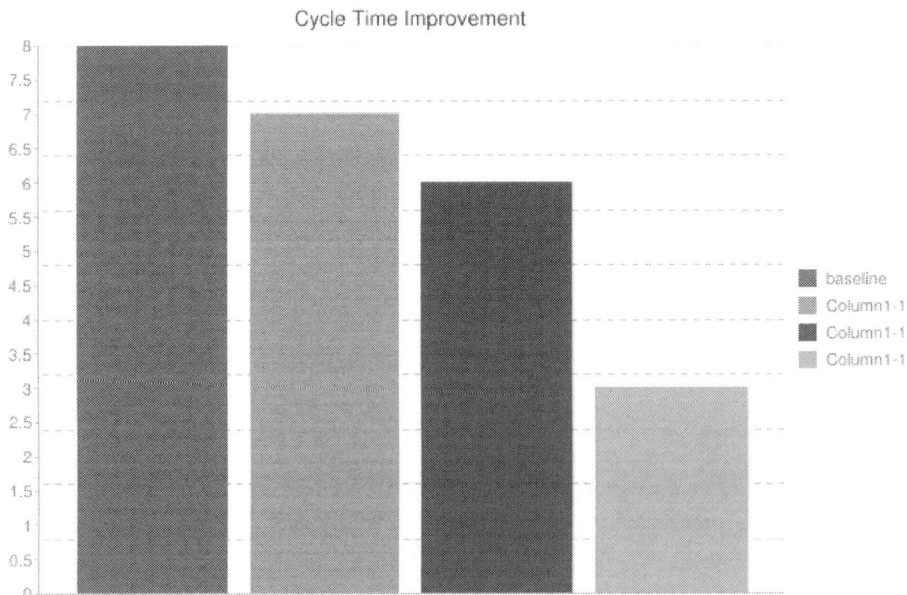

Cycle Time Improvement

Another solution that would reduce cycle time is to increase the capacity of Column 3. To test that scenario, execute the following addStaff command (the difference is the count equals plus three rather than minus three) -

```
<simulation name="Cycle time reduction" >
  <execute>
    <addStaff cycles="50" count="3" optimizeForLowest="cycleTime"/>
  </execute>
  <setup> …
```

The result is significant. Even after a single WIP limit increase in Column 3, the cycle-time is reduced to 4 simulation intervals. Figure 9-5 shows the results of each increase in WIP limit step by step. The purpose of this example is to demonstrate you need to simulate both increasing and decreasing WIP limits when searching for WIP limits that reduce cycle-time. There are good reasons to keep WIP limits as low as possible in order to decrease the variability of cycle-time, but increasing WIP limits can also reduce cycle-time when analyzed for some model configurations.

Figure 9-5
Results of the add staff simulation looking to decrease cycle-time by increasing WIP.

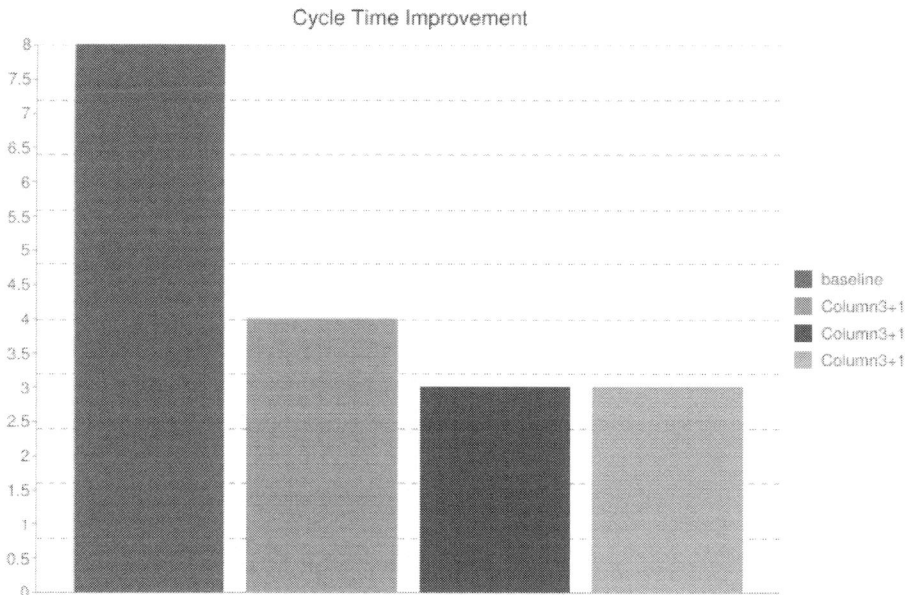

Finding Kanban Board Balance

I call a Kanban board "balanced" when its WIP limits allow for the most throughput from backlog to complete. One way to quickly uncover what WIP limits allow for the best flow through the system is to perform an Add Staff analysis for many suggestions and looking at chart trends. If an `addStaff` analysis was performed looking for the next 20 staff to hire for the model shown in Listing 9-2, the result chart shown in Figure 9-6 is generated. The first three to five suggestions make a large impact on intervals, and then the impact of each suggestion will taper off to minimal impact. I call the point where individual increases in WIP only make small improvements a "balanced board," and it will correspond with lowest queued and empty board positions.

Individual WIP limit increases once the board is balanced and will give small improvements to the number of intervals to complete a project. If you still need to reduce the number of intervals, increasing the WIP limits across the board as a whole (half-again for every column, or double for every column) but maintaining the ratio between column WIP limits of the balanced board is your best (and only) bet.

Figure 9-6
The intervals improvement for an Add Staff analysis looking for the next 20 suggestions.

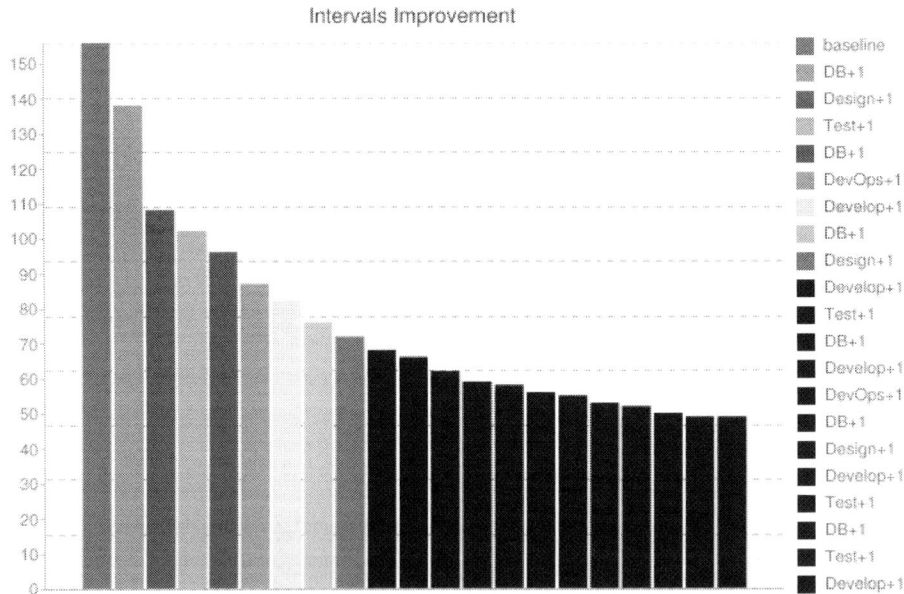

Intervals Improvement

Legend:
- baseline
- DB+1
- Design+1
- Test+1
- DB+1
- DevOps+1
- Develop+1
- DB+1
- Design+1
- Develop+1
- Test+1
- DB+1
- Develop+1
- DevOps+1
- DB+1
- Design+1
- Develop+1
- Test+1
- DB+1
- Test+1
- Develop+1

No More Developers Please – More QA & DevOps Staff!

Software development takes a team (well, all but the smallest of projects). You have seen how you can quickly determine what expertise the next hire should have to make an impact on a project timeline. However, I'll almost guarantee you will be offered more code developers as soon as a project timeline is under pressure. If you trust your model and the outcome of an `addStaff` analysis shows that a few more developer makes the biggest impact, you should listen. But, when it doesn't, and it clearly shows that you need more testing or release operations resources in order to keep pace with the code production, then you should listen and advocate that as well.

If you are using a Kanban process to model your system, make sure you model the staff around your immediate code development team – the more of the system you model, the more you will understand individual impacts. If you have access to prior project data, determine the 90th percentile range of cycle-time in each column, and then model the events that block or add scope to these columns. By modeling more of the development to production process, you open up more staff skills to analysis for increased resources (more WIP). I guarantee if you show your boss a chart like that in Figure 9-2 and Figure 9-3, clearly demonstrating that a designer, a database developer and a tester will decrease project time by 34% you will get that staffing request.

The assumption by the simulation software is that these resources are immediately available, trained and would operate at the same cycle-time estimates as those already on the project. This is a fantasy. Before presenting these numbers to your boss, use the following process to account for new staff ramp-up time –

1. Model the current team and forecast a date.

2. Perform an Add Staff analysis for double the number of staff you think you need.

3. Look at the reduction of intervals after each suggestion, and ignore any that offer < 5% improvement over the baseline (unless even that 5% is important to you).

4. For the suggestions you accept, increase the Wip's in the model to match the suggestions.

5. Increase the `estimateHighBound` for each suggested column by the amount of extra time you think the new staff will take to do the work. For example, if the current tester says her 95th percentile bound is 2 days, ask her what it would have taken her on her first day of work – 4 days? Put the `estimateHighBound` at the new estimate or somewhere between the original and the "first day" estimate to account for the current skilled staff.

6. Perform a `forecastDate` with the new model and calculate the difference between this date and that determined in Step 1.

When making the pitch for more staff, show how you decided what the next hires should be, using the chart showing the impact of each addition. To communicate the impact, use the `forecastDate` simulation to derive the improvement number rather than saying "we will take 34% of time out of the schedule with these two hires." Once these new hires are on-board, remember to monitor the actual cycle-times in their columns and quickly change the model if they diverge from your estimate.

Demonstrating More Staff Equals Less Project Cost

Some models will demonstrate that adding more team members and finishing quicker is cheaper than staying at current staff levels. If WIP limits are unbalanced and there is high empty and queued board positions, fixing the staff imbalance with a few targeted hires will be more cost effective than laboring through with the current board configuration. This can save cost substantial if the resources are contracted or can be re-deployed to another project when this one is complete.

We first encountered an example of this in Chapter 2 where we went through a project scenario. The scenario was that an existing team was going to take on a new project and the initial Kanban board WIP limits are used as a starting point. However, the new project has a different balance of user-interface work and design work than the project the team is coming from, and this can be uncovered by simulating the new projects backlog.

Here is the process to explore whether adding more staff will decrease staff costs in delivering a project –

1. Model the new project backlog. Pay specific attention to categorizing the backlog into specialties (for example, UI heavy, DB heavy, server-side heavy) stories, and column cycle-time overrides (see Chapter 6 for ways to describe a backlog of work).

2. Count the number of staff required to fulfill the duties of each WIP limit and calculate the cost per work day of that many staff. If they are outsourced, that is pretty easy, for internal staff come up with a formula to get a cost per day (I used (avg. salary / 52 / 5) x staff).

3. Perform a `forecastDate` simulation and capture the date that matches the likelihood you are comfortable with; I use the date closest to 95%. For example, the following command -

    ```
    <execute deliverables="Must-Haves" dateFormat="ddMMMyyyy">
      <forecastDate startDate="01Oct2011" intervalsToOneDay="1"
    workDays="monday,tuesday,wednesday,thursday,friday" costPerDay="2700"/>
    </execute>
    ```

    produces the result snippet of (other results removed for clarity) -

    ```
    <date intervals="84" workDays="84" date="27Jan2012"
        likelihood="93.60 %" cost="$226,800.00" />
    <date intervals="85" workDays="85" date="28Jan2012"
        likelihood="98.00 %" cost="$229,500.00" />
    ```

4. Perform an `addStaff` analysis for many people, and look at the chart produced (an example is shown in Figure 9-6). Take as many suggestions as you consider appropriate and update the column WIP limits in your model. For example, the command -

    ```
    <addStaff count="3" cycles="250" />
    ```

    produces the chart -

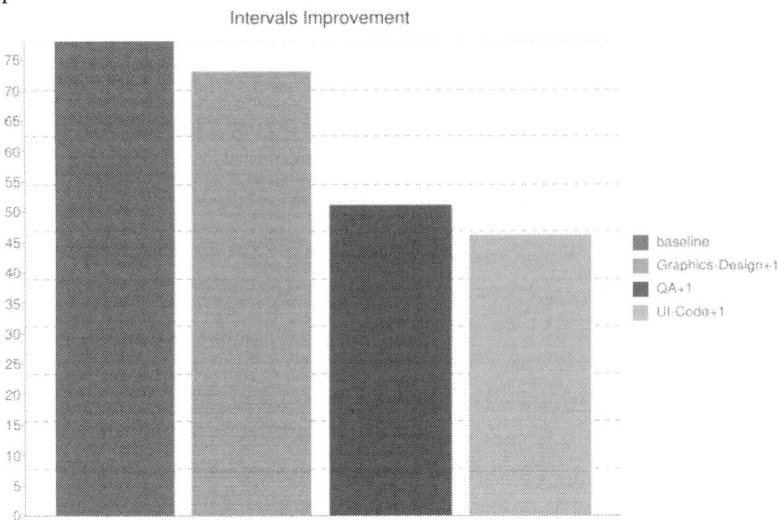

5. Calculate a new cost per day accounting for the increase in staff. In this case, I'll accept adding 2 resources, a graphics designer and a QA engineer. This increases the cost per day from $2700 to $3461.

6. Perform a `forecastDate` command with the new model. For example, executing the following command –

   ```
   <forecastDate cycles="250" startDate="01Oct2011" intervalsToOneDay="1"
   workDays="monday,tuesday,wednesday,thursday,friday" costPerDay="3461" />
   ```

   produces the result snippet of (other lines removed for clarity) -

   ```
   <date intervals="55" workDays="55" date="17Dec2011"
         likelihood="95.60 %" cost="$190,355.00" />
   <date intervals="56" workDays="56" date="20Dec2011"
         likelihood="97.60 %" cost="$193,816.00" />
   ```

7. Calculate the saving of adding two staff by subtracting the results in step 6 from that in step 2:

   7 staff (original team): 28th January 2012 for $229,500
   9 staff (new team structure): 20th December 2011 for $193,816

This isn't a contrived example (well it is, but it is also a common occurrence found looking at many real-world models). There will be many models that have an imbalance in resourcing that causes the forecasted date to be longer than it can be by addressing WIP limits and staffing the project accordingly. In addition to the cost savings, there may well be a revenue upside by the faster time to market allowing sales to be earned earlier. In the example we just worked through, revenue for January can also be counted as an upside to adding more staff and completing the project earlier.

Summary

This chapter has shown how to analyze Kanban projects to find and leverage staff resource opportunities. The ability to model a software project and perform what-if scenarios on resourcing and cost changes makes informing others and getting approval to make changes easier than ever before.

Chapter 10
Sensitivity Analysis

Understanding what factors most impact delivery date and cost is a fundamental skill needed in good software development managers. By modeling a software development project we can determine what input factors cause the most impact of the simulated results, quickly showing our next opportunity for improvement.

Performing a Sensitivity Analysis

Sensitivity analysis is the process of determining what input variable of a model causes the most change in the output results. When analyzed using SimML, the results are shown as an ordered list of input variables, from the ones causing the greatest impact to the ones causing the least. This chapter shows how to perform and how to interpret the results of a sensitivity analysis.

Sensitivity analysis is performed by adding a sensitivity section to the execute SimML element, in the format –

```
<simulation name="Sensitivity Analysis" >
  <execute>
    <sensitivity cycles="250"
                 sensitivityType="intervals"
                 occurrenceMultiplier="2"
                 estimateMultiplier="0.5"
                 sortOrder="descending" />
  </execute>
  <setup>
    ...
  </setup>
</simulation>
```

The `cycles` attribute is the number of simulation cycles to execute and average when finding the baseline and impact of each event occurrence rate or estimate. Depending on the number of events being analyzed, this analysis can take considerable time to complete (a few minutes is not uncommon). Best practice is to start with a low number of cycles to quickly determine if one event is by far the most impactful, and only increasing cycles if two or more event impacts are very close in magnitude. The more simulation cycles, the more certain you will be in the average values used to determine the difference in results between sensitivity analysis tests.

Sensitivity Analysis changes the input variables in a controlled fashion and measures the result of a simulation. The `sensitivityType` attribute is the result value that is measured. The default for a Lean/Kanban project is simulation intervals, and the default for an Agile/Scrum project is iteration count (which is the only value supported for Agile and Scrum projects). Other `sensitivityType` values for Lean/Kanban projects are `cycle-Time`, `queued` and `empty`, representing work card cycle-time, average board queued and empty positions respectively. For each sensitivity type, the result impacts will be ordered either from lowest to highest or highest to lowest value of the sensitivity type result value you choose. The `sortOrder` attribute determines whether results are order from most impactful to least impactful, and will need to be set to ascending for a negative test, or descending for a positive test.

The amount each occurrence rate and estimate value is altered during sensitivity tests is determined by the `occurrenceMultiplier` and the `estimateMultiplier` attributes. The one area of confusion when setting these values is that they work in opposite polarities. A higher value of estimate will negatively impact a project because those stories take longer. A higher value of occurrence rate will positive impact a project, because those events will happen less often. Generally, these values will be the reciprocal of each other. For example, when multiplying occurrence rates by 2 to double them (occur half as often), you would multiply estimates by 0.5 to halve the time taken. This means that everything is essentially halved and both impacts improve the outcome (of measuring intervals and iterations – each change will reduce time).

The suggested settings for most scenarios are –

Test Type	estimateMultiplier	occurrenceMultiplier	sortOrder
Negative Impact 10%	1.1	0.9	ascending
Positive Impact 10%	0.9	1.1	descending
Negative impact 50%	2	0.5	ascending
Positive Impact 50%	0.5	2	descending

The strategy for running sensitivity tests is to make the largest change possible to each value that doesn't create an invalid situation. Most invalid situations come when multiplying a value and having that value become zero or less than zero. Another invalid situation can also be created by too small a change meaning values are rounded to the same value they were originally. By running the four suggested settings and confirming the results are in agreement as to what events are causing the most impact, you will avoid any single problem.

Table 10-1 shows all attributes for the sensitivity section.

Table 10-1
All available attributes for the sensitivity section.

Attribute	Type	Description
cycles	integer (mandatory)	The number of simulation iterations performed as part of this simulation. Must be > 0.
sensitivityType	intervals (default), iterations, cycleTime, queued, empty	The result value to measure impact during testing. For example, if "intervals" are chosen, each analysis will find the impact of a change on simulation intervals. The default is intervals if omitted for Lean/Kanban projects. Agile/Scrum projects must use Iterations (it

		is the only one that makes sense)
estimateMultiplier	number (mandatory)	The value to multiply original estimate values by to determine the new test value. Can be a value < 1 for positive testing, or > 1 for negative testing.
occurrenceMultiplier	number (mandatory)	The value to multiply original occurrence rate values by to determine the new test value. Can be a value < 1 for negative testing, or > 1 for positive testing. (Remember: bigger occurrence rate values mean events occur less often)
sortOrder	ascending (default), descending	The order the difference between baseline and each test for the value chosen in sensitivityType to be listed. Depending on whether performing negative or positive testing, this value needs to be changed to make sure the most impacted test is listed first (tip: use ascending for negative testing, use descending for positive testing).

Understanding the Sensitivity Analysis Results

The results of a sensitivity analysis is a list of tests ordered by the impact they had on the `sensitivityType` attribute result measurement. Each individual test is nested within a `tests` section, as shown in Output 10-1.

Output 10-1

Example tests section with one of many test sections. This test is for an estimate change, notice the original and new estimate boundaries.

```
<tests>
  <test index="0" type="Column" name="UI-Code"
changeType="Estimate"
intervalDelta="-6.192" cycleTimeDelta="-1.448"
emptyPositionsDelta="-0.267" queuedPositionsDelta="-0.052"
originalOccurrenceLowBound="0" newOccurrenceLowBound="0"
originalOccurrenceHighBound="0" newOccurrenceHighBound="0"
originalEstimateLowBound="1" newEstimateLowBound="0.5"
originalEstimateHighBound="3" newEstimateHighBound="1.5">
...
</tests>
```

There are multiple tests executed as part of a sensitivity analysis. The tests performed during analysis are:

1. *Defect occurrence rate*: each defect's occurrence rate is changed and tested.
2. *Added scope occurrence rate*: each added scope's occurrence rate is changed and tested.
3. *Blocking event occurrence rate*: each blocking event's occurrence rate is changed and tested.

4. *Blocking event estimate*: each blocking event's low bound and high bound estimate is changed and tested.

5. *Kanban columns*: Each Kanban column's low bound and high bound estimate is changed and tested.

After each individual test, the occurrence rate and estimates are returned to their original value, so each test isolates only a single input criteria for impact analysis each test. The specific test type is recorded in the `type`, `name` and `changeType` attributes within each test. This can be seen in Output 10-1 and Output 10-2 that show a change to a column's estimate values in the first case and a change to a defect's occurrence rates in the latter case.

Output 10-2

This sensitivity test result is for an occurrence change. Notice the `changeType="Occurrence"` *and the original and new occurrence values.*

```
<tests>
  <test index="1" type="Defect"
name="UI Defect" changeType="Occurrence"
intervalDelta="-4.14" cycleTimeDelta="-0.345"
emptyPositionsDelta="0.081" queuedPositionsDelta="-0.1"
originalOccurrenceLowBound="2" newOccurrenceLowBound="4"
originalOccurrenceHighBound="3" newOccurrenceHighBound="6"
originalEstimateLowBound="0" newEstimateLowBound="0"
originalEstimateHighBound="0" newEstimateHighBound="0">
...
</tests>
```

The HTML report for a sensitivity test puts the results in a tabular format. Each test is listed as a column, with the most impactful listed first (if the `sortOrder` attribute is set correctly). Figure 10-1 shows an example sensitivity analysis report that is launched when the Launch button is clicked after a sensitivity analysis is executed using the Kanban and Scrum Visualizer application.

Figure 10-1
HTML result table for a sensitivity analysis.

	UI-Code	UI Defect	Graphics-Design	Server-Side Code	QA	Spec question (awaiting answer)	Spec question (awaiting answer)	Server-Side Defect	Block testing (environment down)	Block testing (environment down)
Object Type	Column	Defect	Column	Column	Column	BlockingEvent	BlockingEvent	Defect	BlockingEvent	BlockingEvent
Change Type	Estimate	Occurrence	Estimate	Estimate	Estimate	Estimate	Occurrence	Occurrence	Estimate	Occurrence
Interval Delta	-6.192	-4.14	-3.256	-2.06	-1.084	-1.056	-0.772	-0.616	-0.42	-0.34
Cycle-time Delta	-1.448	-0.345	-0.132	-1.487	-1.341	-0.049	-0.015	-0.092	-0.339	-0.219
Empty Positions Delta	-0.267	0.081	-0.37	0.524	0.613	-0.154	-0.143	0.173	0.206	0.142
Queued Positions Delta	-0.052	-0.1	0.496	-0.091	-0.141	0.067	0.066	-0.024	-0.058	-0.035

Proving Quality Code Counts

One application of impact analysis is to demonstrate to your team the importance of writing quality code and taking some extra time testing it yourself before sending it on to QA. Everyone agrees the effort and time taken to turnaround a fix for a defect gets longer the further down the release process it reaches, but for many developers, seeing is believing.

The scenario is common – you are seeing more defects reaching the QA team that should have been spotted by the developer during coding time. This causes work to be sent back that disrupts the team's flow and delays releases. The solution is to demonstrate to the developers what the equivalent extra time spent during development would be, to match the current impact of the excessive defects leakage. You and your team might be stunned at just how long that time offset is – so much so, that the developers enthusiastically use a fraction of that time in testing their work and your project encounters a net improvement – win –win.

To prove the impact of these defects, follow this process –

1. Using actual data, update your model to have a defect entry that matches measured occurrences.

2. Perform a forecast date simulation and record the entry that is closest to $95^{%}$ likelihood (it can be any likelihood value, but this is the one I use).

   ```
   <date intervals="142" workDays="142" date="18Apr2012"
        likelihood="97.20 %" cost="$491,462.00" />
   ```

3. Comment out (or temporarily delete) the defect from the model and run the same forecast date simulation recording the entry closest to 95% likelihood.

   ```
   <date intervals="111" workDays="111" date="06Mar2012"
        likelihood="96.40 %" cost="$384,171.00" />
   ```

4. Emphasize the date and cost difference between step 3 and step 2. This is the cost difference if all defects of this type were eliminated, and represents the worse-case scenario.

5. Double the time estimates for the relevant development column (in all places of the backlog and column definitions) and execute another forecast date simulation to show that even a *doubling of development time* doesn't cause the same impact as the current defect rate.

   ```
   2x:  <date intervals="122" workDays="122" date="21Mar2012"
            likelihood="95.20 %" cost="$422,242.00" />
   ```

6. Emphasize that even doubling the time spent in the development work column there would still be a net saving of $65,000 and almost 1 month quicker in delivery date. The estimates in the case were moved from 3 to 5 days to 6 to 10 days. Suggest that if every developer spent even a single extra day checking their work and getting a business owner to review the work on the developer machine, a major impact could be seen.

This scenario was taken from a real-world project. Small UI defects were being found in every story, often due to multi-browser issues and accessibility flaws in the code. By demonstrating to the developer the actual impact of the round-trip of these defects from the QA team, the developers grabbed a QA person before checking-in code, and installed all the other internet browsing applications onto their development machines for testing. The results were dramatic; but no amount of conversation during the stand-up meetings or retrospectives was getting any traction – seeing the impact visually and on release date made the developers feel the pain.

The previous scenario was for a Kanban project, but similar approaches can be used for Agile/Scrum projects. For scrum projects, follow the same process but double the story-points of the original backlog items when forecasting with the defect in question removed from the model. The results will be just as startling.

Summary

Modeling and simulation offers a platform for performing rapid what-if analysis on a project. The ability to measure the impact of each event in a model on the results gives valuable insight into what opportunities can be leveraged to bring-in a release date.

By using the built-in impact sensitivity analysis tools, or by manually making changes and re-running a forecast, you can find and demonstrate the cost and impact of events and use this to change behavior or get the resources needed.

Chapter 11
Analyzing Real-World (Actual) Data

Before a project begins, expert estimates are the only information available to build a model. Once a project is ongoing, you should be refining the estimates in the model with intelligence from measured data. This chapter describes how to decide what data is valuable to measure, and how to take that actual data and convert that into model input parameters in order to make your model more accurate.

What to Measure – Determining Value of Information

Actual data comes from a variety of sources. As part of managing a project you should put in place systems that record actual data early in the project so as not to lose the ability to leverage this data in making your model more accurate. Ideally, every input parameter for your model should have a corresponding actual measurement system once a project begins and you should be constantly monitoring and comparing these against the model's values. Divergence will occur, and this is an opportunity to learn and improve the model.

Data capture doesn't need to take a lot of extra work for the team, and it definitely shouldn't impact delivery timeframes by adding more work to the teams backlog. If it does take time from the teams work schedule, make sure to add an Added Scope event to the model and measure its cost and time impact, then consider if it is worth the effort. Unless it actively improves a model's accuracy for an input variable that has high impact, then stop the data capture workload.

When determining what actual measurement data sources to capture and analyze, run a sensitivity analysis on the model. Start from the most influential event or estimates in the impact results, and actively stop any overhead that the team has for capturing actual data for factors that have very little impact on schedule or cost. Constantly re-run the sensitivity report, because as the model changes over time, so does the order and impact of different events on forecasts. What you manage at the start of the project may not be the best set of factors to manage at the end of the project.

It's important that a model draft is quickly built and used to determine input estimate sensitivity. Working from the ordered list of impact, find or institute a way to get actual data for the most influential inputs. For example, Figure 11-1 shows the results of a sensitivity analysis. Finding a source of actual data from previous projects or from the actual cycle-time for UI-Coding specifically and the occurrence rate of UI-Defects for the first few weeks of project work will help improve the model for the two biggest impacting input estimates. Spending time on any estimate that will eventually cause less than an iteration or simulation interval isn't the best use of anyone's time. I am making the assumption that you are confident that your estimates cover the 90th percentile range of potential actuals, and if a doubling of an occurrence rate or estimate still doesn't make a significant impact, you don't need to monitor these as closely.

Figure 11-1
HTML result table for a sensitivity analysis.

	UI-Code	UI Defect	Graphics-Design	Server-Side Code	QA	Spec question (awaiting answer)	Spec question (awaiting answer)	Server-Side Defect	Block testing (environment down)	Block testing (environment down)
Object Type	Column	Defect	Column	Column	Column	BlockingEvent	BlockingEvent	Defect	BlockingEvent	BlockingEvent
Change Type	Estimate	Occurrence	Estimate	Estimate	Estimate	Estimate	Occurrence	Occurrence	Estimate	Occurrence
Interval Delta	-6.192	-4.14	-3.256	-2.06	-1.084	-1.056	-0.772	-0.616	-0.42	-0.34
Cycle-time Delta	-1.448	-0.345	-0.132	-1.487	-1.341	-0.049	-0.015	-0.092	-0.339	-0.219
Empty Positions Delta	-0.267	0.081	-0.37	0.624	0.618	-0.154	-0.143	0.173	0.206	0.142
Queued Positions Delta	-0.052	-0.1	0.496	-0.091	-0.141	0.067	0.066	-0.024	-0.058	-0.035

   To put a dollar value on the risk of not accurately modeling an estimate, perform a forecast date simulation with that aspect set to half and then doubled from its original state. This will give you a range of dollar amounts of cost and a date range of delivery for the risk of being off by half either in a positive or negative direction. If it is a high impact event, then this number will be significant; significant enough to garner support for spending extra time in estimation analysis, and for time spent measuring and mining actual data to corroborate that estimate early.

Getting Actual Data

Having arrived at a short-list of what data estimates are the most valuable to improve the model estimates with the use of actual data, finding a low-impact way of monitoring actuals is the next task. Existing management tools that are in-place for day-to-day project management will likely be the source for most data, but there are hundreds of different tools being used. This book isn't going to attempt to cover them all, but will show a few examples to demonstrate the techniques you can adapt.

Iteration Story Points Range

For Agile/Scrum projects, the number of story points completed per iteration is a major factor in model accuracy. Fortunately this is one of the more obvious measures and likely to already be captured by the team in a spreadsheet or computerized tool. Make sure that you capture a snapshot of the data each iteration if the tool used to manage it doesn't capture it over time. What you need is a set of numbers, team size (count of staff), and influencing factors for each iteration, for example, use a spreadsheet as shown in Table 11-1.

Table 11-1

Recording Story Points per Iteration Actual Data

Iteration	Date Start	Team Size	Points Completed	Influencing Factors

Some teams have a target for points to complete for each iteration, and this is the value recorded. From a modeling perspective, this isn't useful. You need to find the actual number of completed story points, not those half completed, or almost completed – you need fully completed.

Iteration story points completed are influenced by many factors. The team gets more experienced, more backlog items are similar to others already completed, staff are added or removed – each of these factors causes variability over time for the story point completion rates. Spend some time in each iterations retrospective asking the team to give opinions as to what factors most influenced this iterations story point completion rate. Look for added scope and blocking events that might need adding to the model; you want to make sure you don't double-count the impact by decreasing the story point per iteration estimates and also add work through an added scope event.

I also suggest capturing the team size over time. This often doesn't get recorded in any specific tool, and helps you understand why the number of completed points changed over the timeline of the project. You will be asked "why the increase" sometime down the road, and this spreadsheet will help you remember.

Tip – Version Control Your Models

Models should be updated constantly. Keep all versions of your model over time as it changes by using a version control tool, or by saving out copies of the model with a date in the filename. At a minimum, the backlog size changes over time (work is completed), and the team size changes, causing different cycle-times and story-point completion over the life of the project. Make sure you capture the history of these in order to see how and why the model forecasts evolved over time.

Column Cycle-Times

Lean/Kanban project use cycle-time as the measurement of how long each work item spends in a particular column. The measurement you want to institute is the time between when a work story card first enters a column to the time it moves to the next column or to complete.

You want to confirm that you do NOT count the blocked time. Most automated systems will include blocked time as the cycle-time for a column, but if we have accounted for this blocking time using a Blocking Event model entry, there would be double-counting the time taken. Your choices are to delete the blocking event entry and use the enlarged cycle-time estimate, or remove the cycle-time impacted by blocking from the actual data analyzed. Figure 11-2 shows a scatter-plot of the cycle-times for a Kanban column. There are two distinct groups of values, the ones in the top-right-most(B) box are likely impacted by a blocking event. Use the range of the values in the bottom-left-box(A) for the column estimates, and use the difference between the box A and B range of values as the estimate for the blocking event (this is demonstrated very shortly in the section Finding the 90th Percentile Range).

Figure 11-2
Scatter plot of cycle-time. The values in the box B are impacted by a blocking-event.

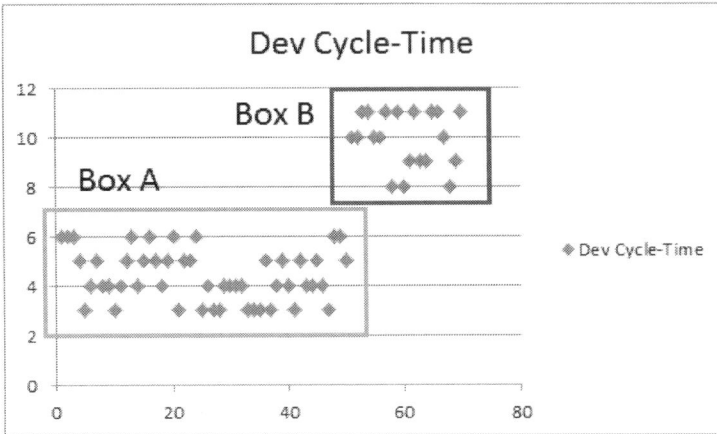

Tip – Blocking Event Occurrence Rate

In addition to giving the boundaries of cycle-time, Figure 11-2 also gives you the occurrence rate of the blocking event causing the increase in cycle-time. Count the number of scatter-plot entries within the box and divide by the time period being measured. This gives a measured occurrence rate. Pick different time periods to get an upper and lower bound.

Defect Occurrence Rates

Bugs are tracked in different ways by teams, some use software, some use a specific color post-it note on a whiteboard. You need to measure the rate these are created however they are stored.

To determine the occurrence rate for all defects, setup a system or a query in the application managing the defects to capture the date a defect is created. You also need to measure the amount of story cards that pass completion (of that column or into the completed work list) over the same period of time. This allows you to calculate the percentage of cards that generate a defect.

For example, the measured numbers from actual data show that –

- QA found 5 defects last month that were sent back to the Dev team.
- 10 Cards passed into QA in total during the last month.

This is a defect rate of 5 cards in 10, which equates to a defect rate of 50% or 1 defect for every 2 story cards. The defect model would look like (Column 4 is QA, column 3 is Dev) -

```
<defect columnId="4" startsInColumnId="3"
        occurrenceLowBound="2" occurrenceHighBound="2">
        Bug found in QA</defect>
```

Scrum defects are similar, but often can be represented more accurately by looking at the number of completed story points versus the number of defects added over a time period. For example, the measured numbers from actual data show that –

- QA created 5 defects last iteration that were sent to the backlog.
- 50 story points of work were completed last iteration.

This is a defect rate of 5 defect stories for every 50 completed story points, or 1 defect for every 10 story points. The defect model in this case would be –

```
<defect  occurrenceType="size"
        occurrenceLowBound="10" occurrenceHighBound="10"
        estimateLowBound="1" estimateHighBound="2" >
        Bug found in QA</defect>
```

Both example shown so far haven't accounted for variability (the `occurrenceLow-Bound` was set to equal the `occurrenceHighBound`). To get the lower and upper boundaries, carry out similar calculations over more time periods to get a set of occurrence rates with a range of values. Use these ranges of values to determine the 5th percentile and the 95th percentile values that can then be added to the model's occurrence rates. We cover how the extrapolate the 90th percentile range now.

Tip – More defects than work!

Sometimes there are more defects than story cards completed over a time period. This is an indicator that the count attribute of the defect should be > 1. You also need to make sure that the size of these defects in cycle-time or story points is defined small enough to make sure the project will finish (if more defect work is being created than work completed, you have a major problem to manage).

Finding the 90th Percentile Range

Throughout this book we have constantly expressed estimated size and occurrence rate in terms of the 90th percentile range. The 90th percentile range is the values that are between the 5th percentile and the 95th percentile of all values. Initially we guess, but after we have actual data, we can and should refine our model.

You might question why we don't just use the entire range of measured values as the lower and upper bound of model entries. The answer is to avoid exaggerating the impact of very rare events. If most defects take 1 to 2 days to fix, but 1 in the last 100 took 5 days to fix, having every defect follow the range from 1 to 5 days would exaggerate their impact by shifting the average higher than actual; the range 1 to 2 days would yield a more accurate simulation result. If you want to account for the outliers, add a specific Blocking Event with the outliers occurrence rate (1 in 100 with a 3 day estimate for this example).

Tip – Must Reads: The Flaw of Averages and The Black Swan

The authors of the books The Flaw of Averages and The Black Swan have strong opinions on how often rare events shape reality. Major events that happen extremely rarely and would be excluded as outliers using a 90th percentile range may well occur in your project and invalidate the model. I'm not saying ignore them, I'm saying make sure that you consider these events and model the impact at various occurrence rates in their own right rather than exaggerating the impact of those rare events for every other defect, blocking event.

In other words - keep each event type distinct so that you can measure their impact explicitly.

You have two main options for calculating the 90th percentile range on a set of data –

1. Use Microsoft Excel or another spreadsheet tool.
2. Use the `summaryStatistics` command in SimML.

Using Excel to Find the 90th Percentile Range

Excel is the common tool of choice for initial exploration of lists of numbers. Finding a given percentile for a range of data is pretty simple using the built-in functions as can be seen here –

```
=PERCENTILE(A2:A71, 0.05)

=PERCENTILE(A2:A71, 0.95)
```

These cell formula's finds the 5th and 95th percentile value of the set of numbers in the cell range A2 to A71. Figure 11-3 shows a scatter-plot of the values in a set of numbers. By using the percentile function the infrequent outliers fall out of the range, with the resulting percentile values being 3 for the 5th percentile and 11 for the 95th percentile.

Figure 11-3
Scatter plot in Excel showing outliers that are removed using percentiles

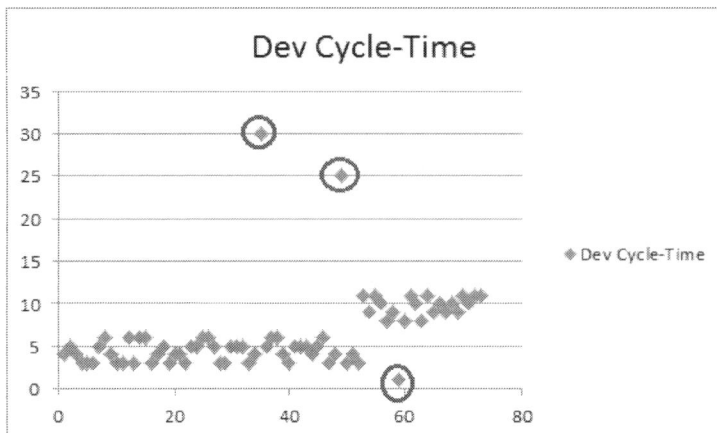

I strongly recommend creating a scatter-plot in Excel to double-check the range you are given. Excel isn't likely to be mathematically wrong, but it is good to understand what outliers are being removed just in case they are a missing blocking event occurrence that can be added to your model.

Figure 11-3 also shows another important factor to model. There are two distinct ranges of numbers in this list. The ones on the left are the normal cycle-time ranges for the column in question. The numbers on the right side are due to the additional time spent as part of a blocking event that occurs 33% of the time (calculated by counting the number of entries in this band by the total number of samples). Listing 11-1 shows how the actual data represented in Figure 11-3 can be modeled. The column estimate is the 90th percentile range of the samples shown on the left side of the scatter plot. The blocking entry estimate was calculated as the step size of the samples on the right. Because the range of the 5th to 95th percentile values in this group was the same as the original column estimate, the lowBound and highBound values were explicitly set to the one value. If those samples had a different range, you should account for its variability.

Listing 11-1

Modeling the impact of a blocking event on the normal cycle-time of a column.

```
<setup>
  <columns>
    <column ...>Design</column>
    <column id="2" estimateLowBound="3" estimateHighBound="6"
            wipLimit="4">Develop</column>
    <column ...>Test</column>
  </columns>

  <blockingEvents>
    <blockingEvent columnId="2" occurrenceType="percentage"
            occurrenceLowBound="33" occurrenceHighBound="33"
            estimateLowBound="5" estimateHighBound="5">
            Block dev event 33% (1 in 3 cards) time</blockingEvent>
  </blockingEvents>
```

Using Kanban and Scrum Simulation Visualizer application

The Kanban and Scrum Visualizer application has built-in functionality for analyzing a set of existing data. The SimML command of summaryStatistics analyzes a set of numbers returning the 5th and 95th percentile values in addition to all of the other summary statistics about that set of data. To execute a summary statistics analysis on a set of numbers, execute the following SimML file -

```
<simulation name="Summary Statistics for Data">
    <execute>
      <summaryStatistics separatorCharacter="\n">
[your data here separated by a new line character between entries]
      </summaryStatistics>
    </execute>
    <setup>
```

```
          </setup>
</simulation>
```

Tip – Copying and Analyzing Data from Excel

If the actual data is currently in Microsoft Excel (or you can get it there), formatting for analysis in SimML becomes easy. Select the data in the column and paste it into the `summaryStatistics` section. Use the `separatorCharacter="\n"` attribute to specify that each data element (row in excel) is separated by a new-line character.

The results from running a `summaryStatistics` command is a results section that is identical to a statistics section in any of the other simulation results we have seen so far. Output 11-1 shows the results generated when the `summaryStatistics` command is executed on the same data that we saw plotted in Figure 11-3. The `fifthPercentile` attribute and the `ninetyFifthPercentile` attributes are the correct boundaries for the 90th percentile range.

Output 11-1

Summary statistic results from the data shown in Figure 11-3

```
<results success="true" elapsedTime="5">
  <summaryStatistics count="73"
minimum="1" average="6.411" maximum="30"
populationStandardDeviation="4.478" sampleStandardDeviation="4.509"
median="5" mode="3"
fifthPercentile="3" twentyFifthPercentile="4"
seventyFifthPercentile="9" ninetyFifthPercentile="11" >
    <histogram>
      <group bin="1" value="1" count="1" />
      <group bin="2" value="3" count="16" />
      <group bin="3" value="4" count="11" />
      <group bin="4" value="5" count="14" />
      <group bin="5" value="6" count="9" />
      <group bin="6" value="8" count="3" />
      <group bin="7" value="9" count="5" />
      <group bin="8" value="10" count="5" />
      <group bin="9" value="11" count="7" />
      <group bin="10" value="25" count="1" />
      <group bin="11" value="30" count="1" />

<chart><![CDATA[http://chart.apis.google.com/chart?chxr=0,0,16|1,1,
30&chxt=y,x,x&chds=0,16&chbh=a&chs=600x400&cht=bvg&chco=3072F3&chd=
t:1,16,11,14,9,3,5,5,7,1,1&chdl=Frequency&chg=0,10&chtt=Histogram&c
hxl=1:|1|3|4|5|6|8|9|10|11|25|30|2:||||Note:+Histogram+is+showing+e
xact+values.|]]></chart>
    </histogram>
  </summaryStatistics>
</results>
```

The results from a `summaryStatistics` command also generates a histogram of the data as shown in Figure 11-4. Although it's not as clear as we saw in the scatter plot of Figure 11-3, the histogram also gives an indication of a skewed data set. This means that if we used the range 3 to 11 for all 73 stories moving through the development column, we would be overstating the cycle-time.

Figure 11-4

Histogram generated from the `summaryStatistics` *command*

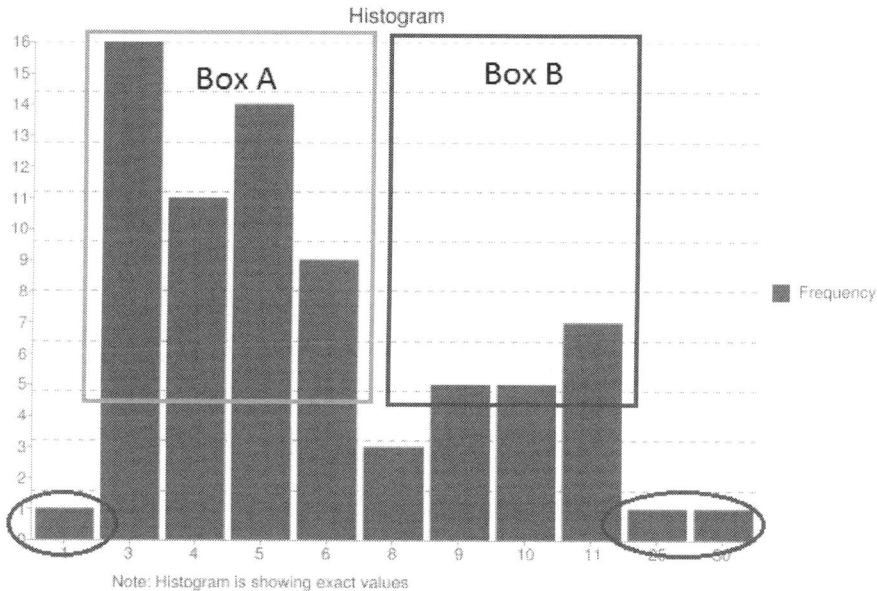

Figure 11-4 shows the outliers to be excluded (because they are above or below the 90th percentile range marked with red ovals. Two distinct sets of data are shown bounded by the Box A and Box B rectangles. On seeing this histogram, look deeper at the original data, and in this case, going back to the Kanban tracking tool, the story cards in the Box B group were impacted by a blocking event. Listing 11-1 shows how this data can be modeled using the histogram results, and also some investigative work on the source of that data.

Summary

Although analyzing actual data is simple in theory, it takes commitment to dig deeper into actual data in order to find the root cause of a number and to model those causes in SimML. That's why I want to stress again, only carry out this work after you have assessed the value of that information and know it is material in impact to the final forecast.

References

Bray, T., Paoli, J., Sperberg-McQueen, C. M., Maler, E., & Yergeau, F. (2008, November 26). *Extensible Markup Language (XML) 1.0 (Fifth Edition)*. Retrieved September 6, 2011, from W3C: http://www.w3.org/TR/xml/

Feynman, R. (1986). *Personal Observations on the Reliability of the Shuttle, Appendix IIF*. NASA Rogers Commission Report.

Grenning, J. W. (2002, April). *Planning Poker or How to avoid analysis paralysis while release planning*. Retrieved September 1, 2011, from RenaissanceSoftware.net: http://renaissancesoftware.net/files/articles/PlanningPoker-v1.1.pdf

Hubbard, D. W. (2009). *The Failure of Risk Management: Why It's Broken and How to Fix It*. Wiley.

Marsaglia, G. (1995). *Diehard Battery of Tests of Randomness*. Retrieved August 26, 2011, from Florida State University: http://www.stat.fsu.edu/pub/diehard/

Mwtoews. (2007, April 7). *Normal Distribution Curve with Standard Deviations*. Retrieved August 24, 2011, from Wikipedia: http://en.wikipedia.org/wiki/File:Standard_deviation_diagram.svg

Taleb, N. N. (2007). *The Black Swan: The Impact of the Highly Improbable*. New York City: Random House.

The Free Dictionary. (n.d.). *Statistics - the definition of statistics*. Retrieved August 20, 2011, from TheFreeDictionary.com: http://www.thefreedictionary.com/dict.asp?Word=statistics

Wikipedia. (n.d.). *Bessel's Correction*. Retrieved August 24, 2011, from Wikipedia: http://en.wikipedia.org/wiki/Bessel%27s_correction

Wikipedia. (n.d.). *Central Limit Theorum*. Retrieved August 26, 2011, from Wikipedia: http://en.wikipedia.org/wiki/Central_limit_theorem

Wikipedia. (n.d.). *Geometric Mean*. Retrieved August 24, 2011, from Wikipedia: http://en.wikipedia.org/wiki/Geometric_mean

Wikipedia. (n.d.). *Harmonic Mean*. Retrieved August 24, 2011, from Wikipedia: http://en.wikipedia.org/wiki/Harmonic_mean

Wikipedia. (n.d.). *Mean*. Retrieved August 20, 2011, from Wikipedia: http://en.wikipedia.org/wiki/Mean

Wikipedia. (n.d.). *Median*. Retrieved August 21, 2011, from Wikipedia: http://en.wikipedia.org/wiki/Median

Wikipedia. (n.d.). *Mode (Statistics)*. Retrieved August 20, 2011, from Wikipedia: http://en.wikipedia.org/wiki/Mode_(statistics)

Wikipedia. (n.d.). *Risk Management*. Retrieved August 19, 2011, from Wikipedia.org: http://en.wikipedia.org/wiki/Risk_management

Wikipedia. (n.d.). *Standard Deviation*. Retrieved August 24, 2001, from Wikipedia: http://en.wikipedia.org/wiki/Standard_deviation

Wikipedia. (n.d.). *Statistical Randomness*. Retrieved August 26, 2011, from Wikipedia: http://en.wikipedia.org/wiki/Statistical_randomness

Appendices

Appendix A – Sample Model for Website Launch

```xml
<simulation name="Website Launch" >

  <execute limitIntervalsTo="1000" decimalRounding="3"
          deliverables="Must-Haves|Everything-Remaining"
          dateFormat="ddMMMyyyy">

    <forecastDate cycles="250" startDate="01Oct2011"
        intervalsToOneDay="1" costPerDay="3461"
        workDays="monday,tuesday,wednesday,thursday,friday"  />

  </execute>

  <setup>
    <columns>
      <column id="1" estimateLowBound="1" estimateHighBound="3"
              wipLimit="2">Graphics-Design</column>
      <column id="2" estimateLowBound="1" estimateHighBound="3"
              wipLimit="2">UI-Code</column>
      <column id="3" estimateLowBound="1" estimateHighBound="3"
              wipLimit="3">Server-Side Code</column>
      <column id="4" estimateLowBound="1" estimateHighBound="3"
              wipLimit="2">QA</column>
    </columns>

    <backlog type="custom"   shuffle="true">
      <deliverable name="Must-Haves">
        <custom name="Small" count="6"
            percentageLowBound="0" percentageHighBound="66" />
        <custom name="Medium" count="4"
            percentageLowBound="33" percentageHighBound="100" />
        <custom name="UI Intensive" count="5"
            percentageLowBound="0" percentageHighBound="100" >
          <column id="1"
                  estimateLowBound="2" estimateHighBound="5" />
          <column id="2"
                  estimateLowBound="3" estimateHighBound="5" />
        </custom>
        <custom name="Server-Side Intensive" count="6"
            percentageLowBound="0" percentageHighBound="100" >
          <column id="3"
                  estimateLowBound="3" estimateHighBound="6" />
        </custom>
      </deliverable>
```

```xml
    <deliverable name="Everything-Remaining">
      <custom name="Small" count="2"
            percentageLowBound="0" percentageHighBound="66" />
      <custom name="Medium" count="3"
            percentageLowBound="33" percentageHighBound="100" />
      <custom name="UI Intensive" count="2"
            percentageLowBound="0" percentageHighBound="100" >
         <column id="1"
                estimateLowBound="2" estimateHighBound="5" />
         <column id="2"
                estimateLowBound="3" estimateHighBound="5" />
      </custom>
      <custom name="Server-Side Intensive" count="3"
             percentageLowBound="0" percentageHighBound="100" >
         <column id="3"
                estimateLowBound="3" estimateHighBound="6" />
      </custom>
    </deliverable>
</backlog>

<defects>
  <!-- UI defects, normally simple fixes -->
  <defect columnId="4" startsInColumnId="2"
        occurrenceLowBound="2" occurrenceHighBound="3">
      UI Defect
   <column id="2" estimateLowBound="1" estimateHighBound="2" />
   <column id="3"
           estimateLowBound="0.5" estimateHighBound="1" />
   <column id="4"
           estimateLowBound="0.5" estimateHighBound="1" />
  </defect>

  <!-- Server-side defects -->
  <defect columnId="4" startsInColumnId="3"
        occurrenceLowBound="3" occurrenceHighBound="6">
              Server-Side Defect
   <column id="3" estimateLowBound="1" estimateHighBound="2" />
   <column id="4"
           estimateLowBound="0.5" estimateHighBound="1" />
  </defect>

</defects>

<blockingEvents>

<!-- Designer blocked waiting for answer from business -->
  <blockingEvent columnId="1"
     occurrenceLowBound="5" occurrenceHighBound="10"
     estimateLowBound="1" estimateHighBound="3">Spec question
  </blockingEvent>

<!-- Testers blocked because environment unavailable -->
  <blockingEvent columnId="4"
     occurrenceLowBound="4" occurrenceHighBound="8"
```

```
                       estimateLowBound="1" estimateHighBound="2">
            Block testing (environment down)
       </blockingEvent>

    </blockingEvents>
  </setup>
</simulation>
```

Appendix B – Date Format String (dateFormat)

Date and time format strings from http://msdn.microsoft.com/en-us/library/8kb3ddd4.aspx

Format specifier	Description	Examples
"d"	The day of the month, from 1 through 31.	6/1/2009 1:45:30 PM -> 1 6/15/2009 1:45:30 PM -> 15
"dd"	The day of the month, from 01 through 31.	6/1/2009 1:45:30 PM -> 01 6/15/2009 1:45:30 PM -> 15
"ddd"	The abbreviated name of the day of the week.	6/15/2009 1:45:30 PM -> Mon (en-US) 6/15/2009 1:45:30 PM -> Пн (ru-RU) 6/15/2009 1:45:30 PM -> lun. (fr-FR)
"dddd"	The full name of the day of the week.	6/15/2009 1:45:30 PM -> Monday (en-US) 6/15/2009 1:45:30 PM -> понедельник (ru-RU) 6/15/2009 1:45:30 PM -> lundi (fr-FR)
"f"	The tenths of a second in a date and time value.	6/15/2009 13:45:30.617 -> 6 6/15/2009 13:45:30.050 -> 0
"ff"	The hundredths of a second in a date and time value.	6/15/2009 13:45:30.617 -> 61 6/15/2009 13:45:30.005 -> 00
"fff"	The milliseconds in a date and time value.	6/15/2009 13:45:30.617 -> 617 6/15/2009 13:45:30.0005 -> 000
"ffff"	The ten thousandths of a second in a date and time value.	6/15/2009 13:45:30.6175 -> 6175 6/15/2009 13:45:30.00005 -> 0000
"fffff"	The hundred thousandths of a second in a date and time value.	6/15/2009 13:45:30.61754 -> 61754 6/15/2009 13:45:30.000005 -> 00000
"ffffff"	The millionths of a second in a date and time value.	6/15/2009 13:45:30.617542 -> 617542 6/15/2009 13:45:30.0000005 -> 000000
"fffffff"	The ten millionths of a second in a date and time value.	6/15/2009 13:45:30.6175425 -> 6175425 6/15/2009 13:45:30.0001150 -> 0001150
"F"	If non-zero, the tenths of a second in a date and time value.	6/15/2009 13:45:30.617 -> 6 6/15/2009 13:45:30.050 -> (no output)
"FF"	If non-zero, the hundredths of a second in a date and time value.	6/15/2009 13:45:30.617 -> 61 6/15/2009 13:45:30.005 -> (no output)
"FFF"	If non-zero, the milliseconds in a date and time value.	6/15/2009 13:45:30.617 -> 617 6/15/2009 13:45:30.0005 -> (no output)
"FFFF"	If non-zero, the ten thousandths of a second in a date and time value.	6/1/2009 13:45:30.5275 -> 5275 6/15/2009 13:45:30.00005 -> (no output)
"FFFFF"	If non-zero, the hundred thousandths of	6/15/2009 13:45:30.61754 -> 61754

	a second in a date and time value.	6/15/2009 13:45:30.000005 -> (no output)
"FFFFFF"	If non-zero, the millionths of a second in a date and time value.	6/15/2009 13:45:30.617542 -> 617542 6/15/2009 13:45:30.0000005 -> (no output)
"FFFFFFF"	If non-zero, the ten millionths of a second in a date and time value.	6/15/2009 13:45:30.6175425 -> 6175425 6/15/2009 13:45:30.0001150 -> 000115
"g", "gg"	The period or era.	6/15/2009 1:45:30 PM -> A.D.
"h"	The hour, using a 12-hour clock from 1 to 12.	6/15/2009 1:45:30 AM -> 1 6/15/2009 1:45:30 PM -> 1
"hh"	The hour, using a 12-hour clock from 01 to 12.	6/15/2009 1:45:30 AM -> 01 6/15/2009 1:45:30 PM -> 01
"H"	The hour, using a 24-hour clock from 0 to 23.	6/15/2009 1:45:30 AM -> 1 6/15/2009 1:45:30 PM -> 13
"HH"	The hour, using a 24-hour clock from 00 to 23.	6/15/2009 1:45:30 AM -> 01 6/15/2009 1:45:30 PM -> 13
"K"	Time zone information.	With DateTime values: 6/15/2009 1:45:30 PM, Kind Unspecified -> 6/15/2009 1:45:30 PM, Kind Utc -> Z 6/15/2009 1:45:30 PM, Kind Local -> -07:00 (depends on local computer settings) With DateTimeOffset values: 6/15/2009 1:45:30 AM -07:00 --> -07:00 6/15/2009 8:45:30 AM +00:00 --> +00:00
"m"	The minute, from 0 through 59.	6/15/2009 1:09:30 AM -> 9 6/15/2009 1:09:30 PM -> 9
"mm"	The minute, from 00 through 59.	6/15/2009 1:09:30 AM -> 09 6/15/2009 1:09:30 PM -> 09
"M"	The month, from 1 through 12.	6/15/2009 1:45:30 PM -> 6
"MM"	The month, from 01 through 12.	6/15/2009 1:45:30 PM -> 06
"MMM"	The abbreviated name of the month.	6/15/2009 1:45:30 PM -> Jun (en-US) 6/15/2009 1:45:30 PM -> juin (fr-FR) 6/15/2009 1:45:30 PM -> Jun (zu-ZA)
"MMMM"	The full name of the month.	6/15/2009 1:45:30 PM -> June (en-US) 6/15/2009 1:45:30 PM -> juni (da-DK) 6/15/2009 1:45:30 PM -> uJuni (zu-ZA)
"s"	The second, from 0 through 59.	6/15/2009 1:45:09 PM -> 9
"ss"	The second, from 00 through 59.	6/15/2009 1:45:09 PM -> 09
"t"	The first character of the AM/PM designator.	6/15/2009 1:45:30 PM -> P (en-US) 6/15/2009 1:45:30 PM -> 午 (ja-JP) 6/15/2009 1:45:30 PM -> (fr-FR)
"tt"	The AM/PM designator.	6/15/2009 1:45:30 PM -> PM (en-US) 6/15/2009 1:45:30 PM -> 午後 (ja-JP)

		6/15/2009 1:45:30 PM -> (fr-FR)
"y"	The year, from 0 to 99.	1/1/0001 12:00:00 AM -> 1
		1/1/0900 12:00:00 AM -> 0
		1/1/1900 12:00:00 AM -> 0
		6/15/2009 1:45:30 PM -> 9
"yy"	The year, from 00 to 99.	1/1/0001 12:00:00 AM -> 01
		1/1/0900 12:00:00 AM -> 00
		1/1/1900 12:00:00 AM -> 00
		6/15/2009 1:45:30 PM -> 09
"yyy"	The year, with a minimum of three digits.	1/1/0001 12:00:00 AM -> 001
		1/1/0900 12:00:00 AM -> 900
		1/1/1900 12:00:00 AM -> 1900
		6/15/2009 1:45:30 PM -> 2009
"yyyy"	The year as a four-digit number.	1/1/0001 12:00:00 AM -> 0001
		1/1/0900 12:00:00 AM -> 0900
		1/1/1900 12:00:00 AM -> 1900
		6/15/2009 1:45:30 PM -> 2009
"yyyyy"	The year as a five-digit number.	1/1/0001 12:00:00 AM -> 00001
		6/15/2009 1:45:30 PM -> 02009
"z"	Hours offset from UTC, with no leading zeros.	6/15/2009 1:45:30 PM -07:00 -> -7
"zz"	Hours offset from UTC, with a leading zero for a single-digit value.	6/15/2009 1:45:30 PM -07:00 -> -07
"zzz"	Hours and minutes offset from UTC.	6/15/2009 1:45:30 PM -07:00 -> -07:00
":"	The time separator.	6/15/2009 1:45:30 PM -> : (en-US)
		6/15/2009 1:45:30 PM -> . (it-IT)
		6/15/2009 1:45:30 PM -> : (ja-JP)
"/"	The date separator.	6/15/2009 1:45:30 PM -> / (en-US)
		6/15/2009 1:45:30 PM -> - (ar-DZ)
		6/15/2009 1:45:30 PM -> . (tr-TR)
"string" **'string'**	Literal string delimiter.	6/15/2009 1:45:30 PM ("arr:" h:m t) -> arr: 1:45 P
		6/15/2009 1:45:30 PM ('arr:' h:m t) -> arr: 1:45 P
%	Defines the following character as a custom format specifier.	6/15/2009 1:45:30 PM (%h) -> 1
\	The escape character.	6/15/2009 1:45:30 PM (h \h) -> 1 h
Any other character	The character is copied to the result string unchanged.	6/15/2009 1:45:30 AM (arr hh:mm t) -> arr 01:45 A

Index

Made in the USA
Charleston, SC
13 November 2013